DIARY OF ATONEMENT
THE CASE FOR GOOD AND EVIL

BART KEEGAN

Diary of Atonement: The case for good and evil
© 2018 Bart Keegan

trabkeegan@talktalk.net
biomediaworx.com/bartkeegan

ISBN (hardcover): 978-1-7364497-0-7
ISBN (paperback): 978-0-9827812-3-4
ISBN (Amazon paperback): 979-8-2649624-4-8
ISBN (ebook, all formats): 978-1-7364497-4-5

Published by
Bio Mediaworx
P.O. Box 1233
Liberty, MO 64069
U.S.A.

All rights reserved. Without limiting the rights under copyright reserved above, no part of this publication may be reproduced, stored in or introduced into a retrieval system, or transmitted, in any form, or by any means (electronic, mechanical, photocopying, recording, or otherwise) without the prior written permission of both the copyright owner and the above publisher of this book.

WORKS

- *Diary of Atonement: The case for good and evil*
- *Poems & Prose of Atonement*
- *Wittgenstein's* Philosophical Investigations: *Identity as Paradox*

CONTENTS

PREFACE 1
DAY 1: IDENTITY AS PARADOX 3
DAY 2: THE THESIS OF ATONISM 7
DAY 3: THE GREEKS 9
DAY 4: THE JEWS 17
DAY 5: CHRISTIANITY 21
DAY 6: ANSELM 29
DAY 7: EVIL 33
DAY 8: CHRIST 39
DAY 9: DESCARTES 41
DAY 10: HUME 53
DAY 11: KANT 63
DAY 12: HEGEL 71
DAY 13: RUSSELL 87

DAY 14: WITTGENSTEIN	101
DAY 15: TC	117
ABOUT THE AUTHOR	119
ABOUT THE DESIGNER	121

PREFACE

Although working with a close understanding of the thinkers and thought systems listed in its Contents, this book has neither an Introduction nor Conclusion, neither any Index nor Bibliography, and makes scarce use of scholarly quotations, references, or sources. Rather does the work stand on its own two feet, its language-games saying themselves. Its thesis is this: that each identity in the story of the world – every case of A = A – is something (or that) than which nothing greater can be conceived, as necessarily a two-faced existence of good and evil.

DIARY OF ATONEMENT

DAY 1: IDENTITY AS PARADOX

The purpose of this first day's Diary work is to explore a thinking to see if identity is paradox, not oneness sense, and, if so, what is meant by 'paradox'.

I begin by seeing the Identity Law equation A = A to comprise identity (signed by =) and non-same cases of A as existents qua ex-istents (out-showings). I see these opposite cases qua non-same cases to coincide as identity (=). This coincidence I see to mean paradox. I shall take as the model for identity-as-existents the duckrabbit figure shown below, the faces of which are the duck and rabbit existents – a duck facing left and a rabbit facing right.

IDENTITY, PARADOX
DUCKRABBIT

=

EXISTENTS, OPPOSITE CASES, QUA NON-SAME FACES

DUCK   RABBIT
A   A

Here: duckrabbit is to duck and rabbit faces: as identity is to non-same existents; as identity (signed in A = A by =) is to A/A cases. This talk distinguishes between identity (paradox) and existence qua existence (the existents, the faces).

Such talk I shall call games-talk, borrowing this idea from Wittgenstein's work, *Philosophical Investigations*.

I shall see it that paradox out pictures (exists) as opposites of whatever kind such that identity as paradox means 'something (or that) than which nothing greater can be conceived' (abbreviated as TC) – a wordage I borrow from Anselm's work, *Proslogion* and which wordage I shall in future Diary work refer to as the Word.

TC, IDENTITY, PARADOX, WORD

CASES OF OPPOSITES

Here: paradox is to faces: as identity is to existents; as identity (signed in A = A by =) is to A/A cases; as coincidence is to coincident cases; as TC is to countless cases of opposites – summed as two. Such is identity as TC, as two-faced.

Before closing the Diary entry for today I shall make mention of my understanding of some cases of the traditional thinking, of identity sense as oneness-only sense.

I see it that, traditionally, Monism (One-ism) is the doctrine that reality consists of identity as a singleness or oneness. For example, it could be said that all things as Many are the One qua water (so an early Greek thinking), or that all things as Many are forms of the one thing called energy (so a current scientific view), or that all things as the Many qua created works of God are in reality the One qua the Lord God (so Jewish Monotheism), or that all things as

DAY 1: IDENTITY AS PARADOX

Many qua the three Persons of the Blessed Trinity – Father, Son, Holy Spirit – are the One qua the Lord God (so Christian Monotheism), or that all things as Many, viz., God and World (Man), are in Christ Jesus as the One qua the one Lord (so Christian Monotheism).

To these received-sense variants of Monism I intend to return in future Diary entries. For today's entry, it simply is noted that Monism, whatever the variant, as with its religious variation, Monotheism of any kind, is a games-talk bespeaking oneness, or singleness, as identity.

Against this, I see such cases of oneness (cases of Monism, cases of Monotheism) to be faces-only of identity, existents-only, and not cases of identity. This sense will unfold as assorted cases of traditional thinking – assorted received-sense language games – are critically tested out against the thesis which I am presenting, viz., that identity (its every case) is paradox.

I conclude this day's Diary work by seeing that since by proposal identity is paradox meaning the wordage, then each identity in the story of the world including the world itself – every case of A = A – is identity as paradox, as TC qua the Word as something (or that) than which nothing greater can be conceived.

TC, PARADOX, EACH IDENTITY IN THE STORY OF THE WORLD

NON-SAME EXISTENTS

From this conclusion, I move next to present today's thesis as a thesis of Atonism, as follows.

DIARY OF ATONEMENT

DAY 2: THE THESIS OF ATONISM

As proposed in yesterday's Diary entry, I shall today formulate as a thesis the thinking so far presented. I call it the thesis of Atonism.

Such thesis is this: in the identity equation A = A the flanking A/A cases as non-same terms are in this sense opposites and these as at once the case, as thereby the case of identity as atonement qua 'at-oncement, signed by =. This is identity as paradox, coincidence, atonement.

This thinking I shall call the thesis of Atonism (atonement-ism). From the word 'Atonism' I shall employ as new coinage: 'atonistically' (adverb) and 'atonistic' (adjective). The sense of these usages will clarify in context as the project proceeds.

Reworded, the thesis is this: that each identity in the story of the world – every case of A = A – is something (or that) than which nothing greater can be conceived, as necessarily a two-faced existence of good and evil. To this talk of identity as necessarily good and evil I shall return in future Diary entries.

Having formulated as a thesis the idea that identity is paradox, or atonement, meaning the wordage, as TC, I shall proceed to test out Atonism against numerous cases of the received thought form of Monism and its religious counterpart of Monotheism, which exploratory testing will be the project for the Diary work from hereon.

To close and in rehearsal: in formulating the thesis of Atonism, I see it that I have formulated the understanding that each identity in the story of the world including the world itself – every case of A = A – is the case of paradox, atonement, TC, the Word as something (or that) than which nothing greater can be conceived. Here, identity exists as countless non-same faces, summed as two qua each not any other.

ATONISM

NON-SAME EXISTENTS

I now move to test out the thesis of Atonism against cases of received-sense games-talk, starting with the language games of the Greeks, as follows.

DIARY OF ATONEMENT

DAY 3: THE GREEKS

For the work of this Diary I shall see it that the Western world philosophical tradition of Monism has two main roots: Greek philosophy and Judeo-Christian biblical thought. For today's Diary entry, I shall focus on exploring – in outline only – the Greeks, viz., the pre-Socratics, Sophists, Plato and Aristotle.

I see the Greek historical thinking to have been this: all things are Water (Thales); or the Boundless (Anaximander); or Air (Anaximenes); or Fire (Heraclitus); or Being (Parmenides); or Man qua Measure (Protagoras); or a mixture of seeds (Anaxagoras); or four roots (Empedocles); or the Form of the Good (Plato); or Substance (Aristotle).

From which games-talk, I see it to include philosophy that is as much a talk of the real One (say, Water, or the Form of the Good) as it is a talk of the real ones (say, the four roots, or the Forms).

PRE-SOCRATIC PHILOSOPHY

THE REAL ONE   THE REAL ONES

Here: duckrabbit is to duck and rabbit faces; as identity is to non-same existents; as atonement is to opposite cases; as Greek philosophy is to the real One and the real ones cases.

Next, I see it that Greek philosophy – from Thales to Aristotle – puts out as Cause-and-effects games-talk. Variant games-talk examples are these: Water as First Cause is all things manifested; the Four Roots as First Causes are all things qua appearances; the Form of the Good is foundational for the Forms; the Form of Beauty participates in all beautiful things; Substance grounds its attributes.

CAUSATION

REAL CAUSE[S]   EFFECTS

Here: duckrabbit is to duck and rabbit faces; as identity is to non-same existents; as atonement is to opposite cases; as causation is to real cause and its effects cases.

I next see it that Greek games-talk bespeaks Monism, albeit of different kinds. Reality as the One (say, Water), or as each one of a plurality (say, a root), or each of the Many qua effects caused by reality, is a singleness-sense, a oneness-sense.

ATONISM

NON-SAME CASES OF MONISM

Here: duckrabbit is to duck and rabbit faces; as identity is to non-same existents; as Atonism is to non-same cases of Monism (the real One, each one of a real plurality, each one of the Many effects of reality).

Next to which, I see it that just as the duckrabbit may be seen fixedly as a duck, as duck-over-rabbit, so Greek games-talk voices the real One over the real ones (and parallels), as follows.

DAY 3: THE GREEKS

DUCKRABBIT

DUCK-OVER-RABBIT

Here: duckrabbit is to duck-over-rabbit face; as Atonism is to real-One-over-real-ones case; as atonement is to Causal-Reality-over-effects case; as atonement is to Primary-over-secondary case.

I see variant games-talk to be that of Identity Law stating of identity that 'it is itself' such that: duckrabbit is to duck-over-rabbit face; as it-is-itself is to it-over-itself cases – where 'it' is given ascendancy (priority status as Primary case) over 'itself' such that (for received games-talk) 'it' signifies identity, with 'itself' as merely a secondary qua reflexive sense.

IT-IS-ITSELF

IT-OVER-ITSELF

Here: duckrabbit is to duck-over-rabbit face; as it-is-itself Identity Law is to it-over-itself case (identity-over-reflection case); as atonement is to Cause-over-effect case.

I further see it that, for the traditional case, Monism qua the One-over-ones case prevails whereas, for Atonism, non-same cases of Monism – One-over-ones and ones-over-One – are given parity of esteem as paradox faces which, by the logic of paradox, process in continual mutual eclipse.

This games-talk presents in the following manner.

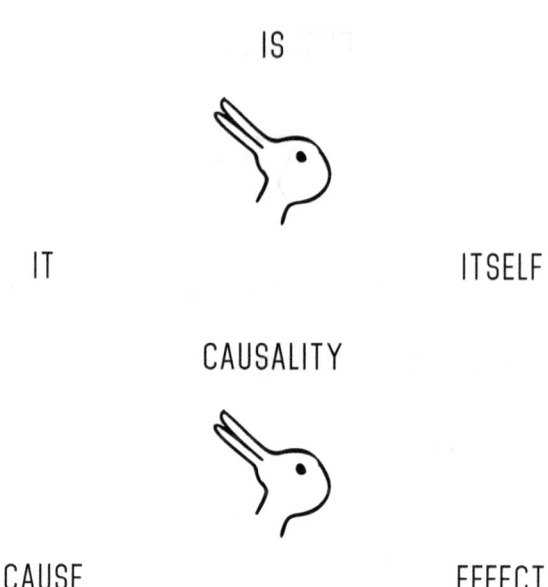

Here: duckrabbit is to duck and rabbit faces; as identity is to non-same existents; as atonement (qua is) is to it and itself cases; as atonement (qua causality) is to cause and effect cases; as atonement is to received-sense identity and reflection cases; as paradox is to subject and mirror-image cases; as eclipse is to eclipsing and eclipsed cases; as Atonism is to non-same cases of Monism.

From which perspective, I see it that Greek philosophical games-talk gives the ascendancy to the One(s) over the Many, causal Reality over its effects. I see this to be the establishment perspective in that it is the perspective which the Greek games-talk establishes as the prevailing mind-set. I see this to be the received wisdom of today called the Western-world thought form.

Further to Greek games-talk to do with the One and Many (ones) distinction, I see it that the Greeks believed in the divinities, which divinities they conceived of in humanistic terms: each god or goddess, like each male or female human, had both admirable and detestable natures (say, courage and cowardice).

Here, then, a distinction is made not only between the divine and the mundane (say, human) but also between good and bad (say, courage and cowardice). Only in this sense is there the Greek recognition of good and evil opposites but these – like the divine and mundane opposites – are at once the case.

DAY 3: THE GREEKS

Relevant games-talk presents as follows.

REALITY

DIVINE   MUNDANE

GOD, GODDESS, MAN, WOMAN

EACH OF GOOD AND BAD NATURES
(SAY, COURAGE AND COWARDICE)

Here: duckrabbit is to duck and rabbit faces; as identity is to non-same existents; as reality is to divine and mundane (including human) natures; as identity (god, goddess, man, woman) is to good and evil (= good and bad) natures (say, courage and cowardice).

I note that in certain Greek games-talk reality is an existent (cf. real One and real ones as existents) whereas in variant games-talk (cf. reality as divine and mundane) reality functions as an identity.

Examples of identity as at once divine and mundane natures is afforded by variant games-talk as these sayings of Thales: things [as cases of matter] are full of gods; the magnet [as a physical or material body] has a soul.

Such games-talk presents as follows.

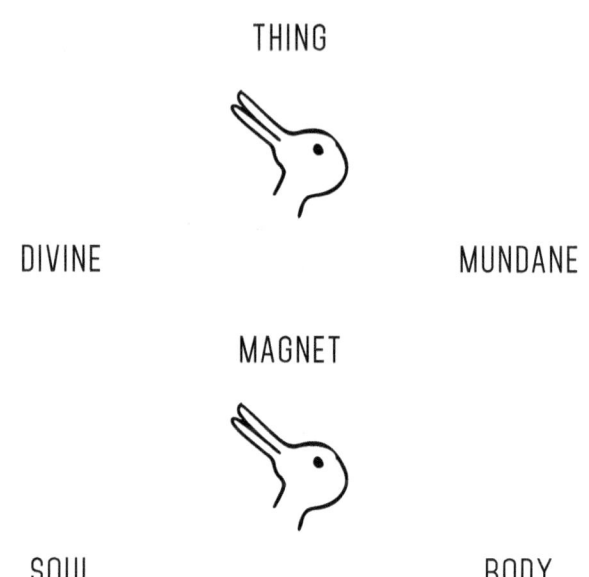

Here: paradox is to faces; as identity is to existents; as atonement is to opposite cases; as thing is to divine and mundane natures; as magnet is to soul and body natures.

To close. I see it atonistically that each identity in the story of the world – every case of A = A – is TC as the Word qua something (or that) than which nothing greater can be conceived, this as paradox, as atonement. Each is at once opposites, as opposite cases qua paradox faces, including as non-same One/ones kinds of Monism, including where the One is ascendant over the ones, also divine and mundane natures, soul and body natures, good and evil natures (= good and bad natures). All such talk of Monism and of ascendant Monism which champions One over Many, I see to characterize the traditional Western world thought form, a root of which is the games-talk of the Greeks.

The Diary work on the Greeks now completed, a next move will be to treat atonistically with the language games of the Jews – the other proposed root of present-day received wisdom – as follows.

DAY 3: THE GREEKS

Note

I see it that neither Plato nor Aristotle gives a telling account of the origin or reason for evil. For Plato there is the Form of the Good participating immediately in the Forms (say, Beauty) and mediately in matter as its very opposite such that matter, in this sense, is evil. For Aristotle there is Substance with attributes of form and matter such that, if form is held to be good, its opposite – matter – is evil, defined as the absence of good. I see Western world games-talk – sprung from the Monism-grounded dualist games-talk of the Greeks, to be this: good is to evil; as form is to matter; as mind is to flesh; as soul is to body; as reason is to sense, as conscience is to appetite; as order is to chaos; as Monism in terms of the One over Many ones is to Monism in terms of the eclipsed Many ones.

To my mind, it must always have puzzled philosophers, from Thales to Aristotle, as to how reality happens to be both good and evil – the puzzle being that if reality is in some respects good (howsoever goodness is defined), why is it not altogether good? Why evil? Or, given evil, why not reality as altogether evil (howsoever evil is defined)? Why goodness? That is: how to make sense of opposites? I see it that the puzzlement arises from the premise that consistency (oneness sense, Monism) is the criterion of rationality, hence of being. In consequence, the 'Problem of Evil' has not to this day being solved, nor, to my mind – given Monism – is it solvable. Rather is it the case (so the thesis of Atonism) that good and evil are at once the case, the case of identity as paradox, as atonement. This is identity qua TC as two-faced, including as good and evil. Of which, much more in due course.

DIARY OF ATONEMENT

DAY 4: THE JEWS

To rehearse from yesterday's Diary work: I see it that the Western world philosophical tradition of Monism has two main roots: Greek philosophy and Judeo-Christian biblical thought. Today I want to focus on the Jewish thought form of Monism, religiously costumed as Monotheism.

I shall see it that whereas Greek philosophical thinking gives out as a varied games-talk such as that of cosmology (all is Water), ontology (all is Being) or anthropology (all is Man as the Measure), Jewish religious thinking gives out as the games talk of theology (sole reality is the one Lord God).

Here: whereas the Greek focus is on the One qua First Cause in philosophical terms, the Jewish focus is on the One qua First Cause personified as God; whereas the Greek prevailing philosophical thought form is Monism, the Jewish prevailing religious thought form is Monotheism.

In either case – Greek or Jewish – the One is by proposal foundational of the Many qua the appearances, creations, or works, of the One. By which received wisdom, the One is the real stuff of identity.

I thus understand Monotheism to be a received-sense language game which says that there is but one God as the One, as Creator of the Many qua all things as the works of God. A case of such Jewish thinking I see to be the Creation and Fall account told out in the biblical Book of Genesis, chapters 2 and 3. I shall explore how this Genesis thinking fits with Atonism, as follows.

The Genesis account tells of the Lord God creating the Garden of Eden containing many trees, two of which are the Tree of Life at the centre of the

Garden and the Tree of the Knowledge of Good and Evil, the only tree the fruit of which Man (Adam and Eve), newly created, is forbidden to eat, on pain of cursed existence and death. A serpent coiled about the Tree of Knowledge successfully tempts Man to taste the fruit in order (for Man) to become like God. Man, in consequence, is cursed and mortalized.

I see it by proposal that variant language games – each bespeaking identity as paradox, as atonement – tell out as follows.

Identity is to non-same existents; as duckrabbit is to duck and rabbit out pictures; as paradox is to different faces; as atonement is to One and Many opposites; as the Lord is to God and Man (Adam and Eve as representatively humankind personifying the manifold world); as Atonism is to Monotheism and apostasy (the dissenting voices of humankind); as knowledge (experience) is to received faith as good qua holiness (sinlessness) and disobedience to that faith as evil qua unholiness (sinfulness); as the Word qua something (or that) than which nothing greater can be conceived is to singular divine nature and manifold mundane nature.

ATONISM, LORD

MONOTHEISM   APOSTASY

By added proposal, I see faithful Man and apostate Man respectively writ large and in metaphysical terms as God and Satan – the respective personifications of good and evil. That the faith and apostasy opposites are respectively writ large as God and Satan I see by proposal to serve the purpose of emphasizing the enormity of the disapproval with which the received-wisdom faith – establishment thinking – views dissension. In this thinking, Monotheism, laying claim to the status of goodness, brooks no apostasy. Apostasy which succumbs to temptation of dissent (the serpent) does so on pain of being cursed as evil (cursed by being outlawed qua earning thoroughgoing disapproval).

DAY 4: THE JEWS

LORD, KNOWLEDGE, MAN

GOD, GOOD,   SATAN, EVIL,
FAITHFUL MAN   APOSTATE MAN

In this games talk, received-sense reality (Monotheism) is oppositely illusion (apostasy) where that reality accords to itself the ascendancy over what it thus deems to be the illusory opposite. The key example is that of God seen to be ascendant over Man. I see this to be the religious games-talk of Monotheism as counterpart to the Greek philosophical games-talk of Monism telling out that the One has ascendancy over the Many ones.

In closing, I note that for the Jews Monotheism was, and is, given the ascendancy over the mind-set of apostasy so that the received thought form of the present Western world, as that of Monism, is for its religious dress Monotheism. By proposal I see it that this received thought form is truncated Atonism: the One, viz., Monotheism, like the Many, viz., the dissenting pluralistic voice of apostasy, is a face-only of atonement, viz., Atonism; received wisdom (Monotheism) is a face-only of identity qua paradox and not identity, which identity is the atonement of the opposites.

This closing games-talk presents in the following manner.

IDENTITY, TC, ATONEMENT, ATONISM

EXISTENT, FAITH   EXISTENT, DISSENSION

Here: paradox is to faces; as identity is to existents; as Lord is to God and Satan cases; as knowledge (experience) is to good and evil natures; as Man is to orthodoxy and apostasy existents; as Man is to establishment Man and anti-establishment Man cases; as Lord is to transcendent God and transcended (fallen) Man existents; as each identity in the story of the world – every case of A = A – is to two-faced existence; as TC as the Word qua something (or that) than which nothing greater can be conceived is to opposite cases (divine and mundane, good and evil, and so on); as Atonism is to One-over-ones and ones-over-One paradox faces in continual mutual eclipse; as Atonism is to non-same kinds of Monism (Monism qua Monotheism and Monism qua each voice of dissent).

I now turn to an investigation of the faith mind-set of Christianity, as follows.

DIARY OF ATONEMENT

DAY 5: CHRISTIANITY

To rehearse from previous Diary work: I see it that the Western world philosophical tradition of Monism has two main roots: Greek philosophy and Judeo-Christian biblical thought. Today I want to focus on the Christian thought form of Monism, religiously costumed as Monotheism.

My focus will not be directly on any text from the New Testament bible. Rather, it will be on received Christian Church doctrines as still preached in Christian churches today. These imply the received Christian theology.

I shall see the feature of Monism – attired in the dress of the traditional thought form of Monotheism – to be evidenced here in that there is the One as the Lord God, also that there is the One as the one Lord Jesus Christ. In either case, the One, or oneness, is the stuff of identity as the stuff of reality. I shall see these to be received variant language games of oneness as identity (the Lord), each game indeed bespeaking oneness but associated with non-oneness games-talk. I shall explore this mixed received-thinking games-talk as follows.

As I understand it, two of the central received-sense, or orthodox, Christian doctrines are these: (1) the doctrine of the Blessed Trinity by which it is held by faith that there is but one Lord God and as three Persons, viz., Father, Son and Holy Spirit; (2) the doctrine of the Incarnation by which it is held by faith that God, in the Person of the Son, incarnated singularly in the historical Lord Jesus as the Christ, as equally God and Man (human natured re: himself, also human natured qua representatively all humankind, indeed representatively all worldliness). Further to these doctrines, there is in **Christian theology** the threefold view of man which holds that man is a composite of **body, soul** and **spirit**.

I propose to call these three cases of orthodox Christian teaching the doctrine of God, the doctrine of Man; the doctrine of Christ. From which proposal, assorted atonistic language games present in the following manner.

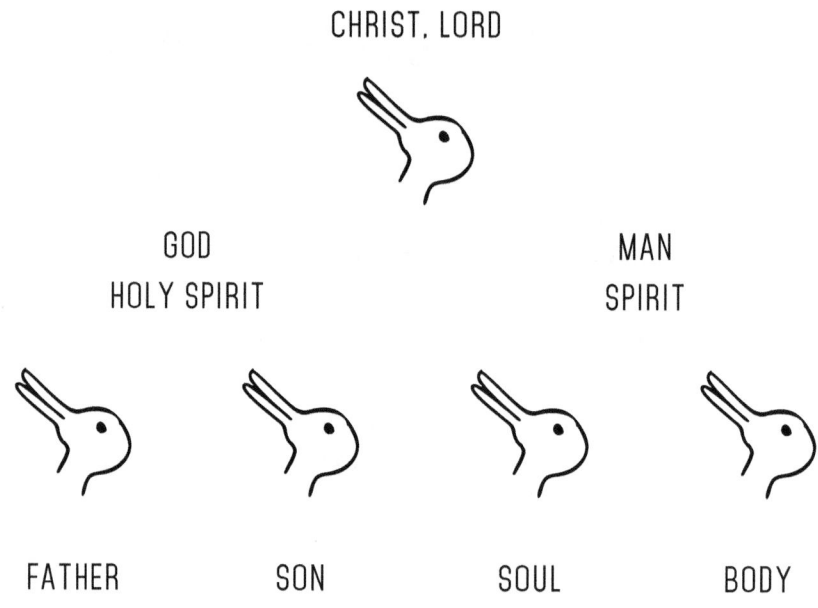

Here: duckrabbit is to duck and rabbit faces; as identity is to non-same existents; as atonement is to opposite cases; as Lord is to God and Man non-same existents; as (re: God) the Person of the Holy Spirit is to Father and Son Persons; as (re: Man) spirit is to soul and body natures (cf. person is to mind and body natures). Opposites, here, include One/Many (singular-soul/manifold-body) cases, also non-same One/One (Father/Son) cases. The topmost duckrabbit summarily represents the Incarnation games-talk of Christ as Godman, the left-side duckrabbit represents the Blessed Trinity doctrine of Spirit as Father and Son; and the right-side duckrabbit represents the teaching the Man is a threefold case, viz., body, soul, spirit. The entire diagram of three duckrabbits represents the case of Jesus the Incarnation – this is Jesus Christ the Lord as the Godman identity qua paradox, or atonement. Within the entire diagrammatic games-talk, comprising variant language games – each bespeaking identity as paradox, as atonement – there are cases of three identities (Lord, Holy Spirit, spirit cf. person) with all other cases being existents qua identity-faces only, not identities.

DAY 5: CHRISTIANITY 23

Further variant languages games, implicit in the above diagrammatic presentation, are as follows.

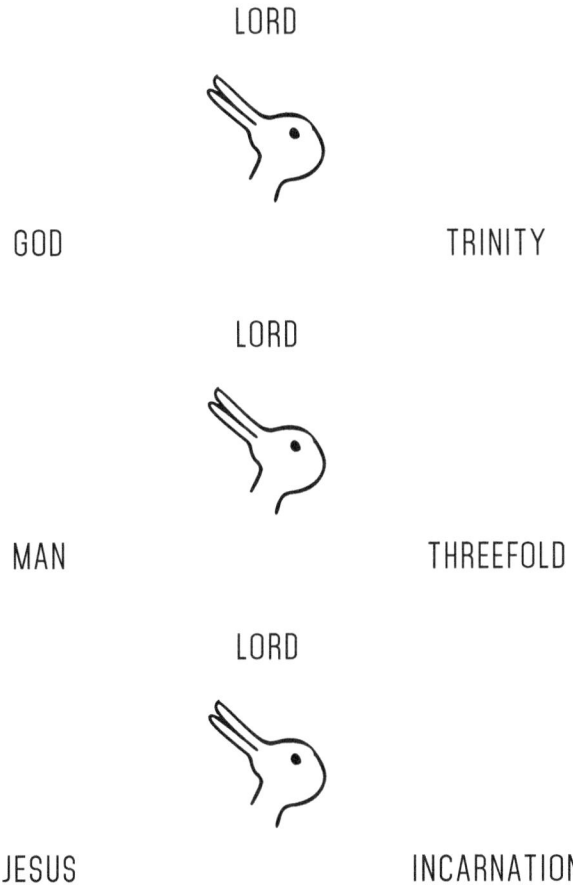

Here: duckrabbit is to duck and rabbit faces; as identity is to non-same existents; as atonement is to One and Many cases; as Atonism is to Monism (Monotheism) and Pluralism cases; as Lord is to God and Trinity (also Man and threefold-sense, Jesus and Incarnation) cases. By which games-talk, the Lordship of God, like the Lordship of Man, is a variant (as a derivative of) the Lordship of Jesus as Christ (identity, paradox, atonement). Again, I note that Lord alone is in each language game the case of identity, the other cases per language game being existents-only qua identity-faces only, not identities.

By this proposal, the overall Christian atonistic games talk presents as follows.

TC, LORD, IDENTITY, PARADOX, ATONEMENT

ALL NON-SAME EXISTENTS

Further exploration of received-sense Incarnation doctrine is this. I understand the orthodox Christian teaching to be a games-talk which voices Jesus Christ not only as sinless qua being the Son of God (S.O.G) but also as sinful qua burdened with world sin in that he is representatively humankind, a Son of Man (S.O.M). I shall see it that this is talk of Man qua Christ as equally Man qua sinless and Man qua sinful, S.O.G and S.O.M, pro-Christ and anti-Christ, Man conforming with the establishment-faith of Monotheism and apostate Man, good Man and evil Man, holy Man and unholy Man, godly Man metaphysicalized as God and ungodly Man writ large and personified as Satan, Man of Creation as Man of innocence and Man of the Fall as Man of guilt, conformist Man applauded to the nth degree by orthodoxy and apostate Man reviled to the nth degree by orthodoxy, transcendent Man qua eclipsing Man and transcended Man qua eclipsed Man, (in mixed games-talk terms) Man qua transcendent God and Man qua transcended (fallen) Satan. The summary games-talk presents as follows.

LORD

GOD   SATAN

The proposed games-talk presents in variant terms in the following manner.

DAY 5: CHRISTIANITY

ATONEMENT, ATONISM

ONE, MONOTHEISM   MANY, OPPONENTS

Here: duckrabbit is to duck/rabbit faces; as identity is to non-same existents; as atonement is to One/Many cases; as Atonism is to Monism (Monotheism) and Pluralism (opponents of Monotheism) cases; as will-to-power is to the voice of orthodoxy and the voices of dissension; as eclipse is to eclipsing/eclipsed paradox faces.

This games-talk gives rise to the following further proposed variant games-talk.

WILL-TO-POWER MAN
CHRIST

RISEN (PEDESTALIZED) MAN   FALLEN (REPRESSED) MAN

PRO-CHRIST,   ANTI-CHRIST,
ASCENDANT ORTHODOXY   OUTLAWED APOSTASY

I see it that, notwithstanding the variants of games-talk bespeaking identity as paradox, as atonement, the overall Christian atonistic games-talk remains the same, presenting in rehearsal as follows.

CHRIST, LORD

GOD   MAN

TC, LORD, IDENTITY, PARADOX, ATONEMENT

ALL NON-SAME EXISTENTS

I see it by proposal that Christianity is not an anti-theism games-talk but is, so to say, the fulfilment of such theism by raising it to the level of atonement logic (atonistic games-talk). Yet, insofar as that orthodox Christian logic pertains to but one identity (the orthodoxly-understood Jesus Christ as Lord), I see it that such orthodoxy is a face-only of identity, not identity itself, which identity is that of all persons and things – as each (in Christian-talk terms) a Lord Jesus Christ. Such expanded atonistic Christian games-talk atones theism and anti-theism (atheism included).

TC, LORD, IDENTITY, PARADOX, ATONEMENT
ECLIPSE

ONE, ORTHODOX CHRISTIANITY   MANY, OPPONENTS,
ECLIPSING   ECLIPSED

DAY 5: CHRISTIANITY

To close. Today's Diary work on Christian Monotheism as a root of present-day Western Monism finds as follows: that each identity in the story of the world – every case of A = A – is identity as paradox, as atonement, TC qua the Word as something (or that) than which nothing greater can be conceived. This is the proposal that each identity is (in Christian games-talk terms) a Christ, as Lord, as the Logos qua Word, the Atonement, existing as opposite cases qua paradox faces, including existing equally divinely and demonically, as good and evil natures. In terms of the Christian games-talk, salvation is the clear-sightedness of one's identity being neither good nor evil, but that than which nothing greater can be conceived – howsoever its existential manifestation.

The Diary work next will take up with a Christian reasoning held by the received mind-set to be what is called an Ontological Argument for the existence of God. How might this sense fit with Atonism?

DIARY OF ATONEMENT

DAY 6: ANSELM

The Diary work for today will explore how the Ontological Argument for the existence of God, attributed to Saint Anselm (c.1033-1109), fits with the thought form of Atonism.

Anselm's reasoning presents as follows (I shall refer to Anselm and the Lord of his Christian faith, respectively, as 'he' and 'He'): Anselm addresses himself not to God but to Lord, requesting that, since it is this Lord that gives understanding to faith, could He give to Anselm, so far as is beneficial to him, an understanding of what he believes. Anselm next states that believers believe that the Lord is something (or that) than which nothing greater can be conceived. I shall abbreviate this wordage to TC. Anselm immediately questions if there is such a Being for the Fool of Psalms 14:1 denies that there is a God. For Anselm, however, no sooner does such Fool hear the TC wordage than he actively understands what he hears, which content of sense is in the Fool's understanding — albeit that this Fool has no understanding that TC exists extra-mentally. For though an object is in the understanding, it is quite another matter as to whether or not it is anything real. An analogy is this: an artwork conceived by the artist is in his understanding but not until or unless he produces that work is it anything real. In which case, the artwork is both in the understanding and exists as something real. Now, for the Fool, since he understands the TC wordage, such TC is at least in his understanding. But clearly, reasons Anselm, TC cannot exist in the understanding alone. For if it be actually in the understanding alone as well as can be thought of as existing additionally in reality, such TC is greater. Therefore, deduces Anselm, the case of the Fool's TC is the case of what is not properly TC — which obviously is impossible. Indubitably, therefore, there exists for Anselm the reasoning believer TC as both in the understanding and in reality. Such is the understanding of the belief. I see the matter as follows. The Fool makes the inequation.

IDENTITY, TC, GOD, IDEAL ≠ IDENTITY, TC, MAN, REALITY

whereas Anselm sees identity (signed below by =) to be TC qua the Lord Jesus Christ of his (Anselm's) Christian confession, to make the equation

EXISTENT, GOD, IDEAL = EXISTENT, MAN, REALITY

whereby TC is the GodMan paradox, the faces of which are ideal-TC and real-TC. The Fool employs the games-talk of secular Monism (each identity a oneness) to reject O.T. establishment-faith qua games-talk of Monotheism (identity as the One). Anselm employs Atonement games-talk to find for both theism games-talk and atheism games-talk as, respectively, orthodoxy and apostasy (God and Man, ideal and real, One and Many) paradoxface existents, not identities.

However, for Atonism, Anselm's Atonement games-talk is orthodox-only Christianity in that it sees an historical Jesus as the sole case of TC (identity, Lord, Christ, GodMan, paradox, atonement). Atonism sees the case to present as properly Christian, as follows.

IDENTITY, ATONISM, TC, LORD QUA CHRIST, PARADOX

IDEAL EXISTENT,	REAL EXISTENT,
MONOSTHEISM, GOD	ATHEISM, MAN

To close. For Atonism, each identity in the story of the world – every case of A = A – is TC (identity, Lord, Man qua Christ, paradox, atonement) as equally One and each one of Many, divine and mundane, ideal and real, perfect and imperfect, good and evil, pro-Christ and antiChrist, God and Satan, O.T. transcendent God (risen qua pedestalized by O.T. establishment faith) and O.T. transcended Man (fallen and outlawed by O.T. establishment-faith decree),

DAY 6: ANSELM 31

godly Man and ungodly Man, orthodox Man (Jewish or Christian) and apostate Man, establishment-adulated orthodox Man and establishment-reviled apostate Man, and so on, for all paired opposites, and necessarily existentially so, by reason of identity logic as paradox logic.

The Diary work on Jewish and Christian religions now done, a problem for each of these is that of evil and it is to this issue that I now shall turn to treat with it atonistically.

DIARY OF ATONEMENT

DAY 7: EVIL

The issue for today's Diary work is this: how does the case of the co-existence of God and evil fit with Atonism?

I begin with what the received mind-set calls "the Problem of Evil." In terms of monotheistic games-talk, I see the problem to be stateable thus: that the concept of goodness personalized and writ large metaphysically as an omni-great God (in power, wisdom, presence, love) is inconsistent with the existence of evil personalized and writ large metaphysically as Satan.

I shall treat with the problem of evil under three heads: the logical problem of evil; the practical problem of evil; and the ontological problem of evil – these as follows.

The logical problem of evil

This is the problem of inconsistency, as stated above. I make answer: There is inconsistency between God and evil for the reason that the two, as opposite cases, are paradox faces. In variant games-talk terms, this reply presents in the following manner.

IDENTITY, LORD, KNOWLEDGE

EXISTENT, GOD, GOOD   EXISTENT, SATAN, EVIL

Here: paradox is to faces; as identity (Lord, knowledge) is to non-same existents (God/Satan, good/evil).

As further variant games-talk: duck is to rabbit; as good is to evil; as God is to Satan; as godly Man is to ungodly Man; as orthodoxy is to apostasy; as establishment Man is to anti-establishment Man; as the voice of decree is to voices of dissent, as One is to Many, as One over Many (ones) is to each one of Many, as the ruling voice of theism is to manifold outlawed atheism, as establishment Monism is to breakaway Monism, as order is to chaos, as wellbeing is to disease, as natural good is to unnatural evil, as law is to crime, as innocence is to guilt, and so on, for all cases of opposites where – by tradition – the first of each pair is given ascendancy over the second of each pair, and where each of the pair is seen to be an identity.

MAN, EXPERIENCE

ORTHODOXY, GOOD   APOSTASY, EVIL

I see it, therefore, that the logical solution to the problem of evil is to see the games-talk of good and evil in atonistic terms, not in traditional monistic terms.

The practical problem of evil

Given good and evil as paradox faces, the fact remains that, from the perspective of goodness, evil is a practical problem. The question for goodness is this: How to eradicate evil? I make answer: by reason of paradox logic, the faces of paradox necessarily process in continual mutual eclipse; accordingly, each face with respect to the other, is both problem and solution.

DAY 7: EVIL

PARADOX

FACES IN CONTINUAL MUTUAL ECLIPSE

Here: paradox is to faces in continual mutual eclipse; as the problem of evil is to good-under-evil and evil-over-good cases; as the solution to evil is to good-over-evil and evil-under-good cases; as eclipse is to eclipsing face over eclipsed face and eclipsed face under eclipsing face cases; as duckrabbit is to duck-over-rabbit and rabbit-over-duck ever interchanging cases. Whatever the games-talk variant, the practical problem of evil, as with its solution, is an existential matter. Each face, as a practical problem for the other, is practically solved by the other.

The ontological problem of evil

This is the problem of how there can be TC qua TC (identity as such identity) given that one of its faces is evil. The question is this: Does not this evil count as a blemish such that TC is not TC – identity is not identity, being is not being, A (in A = A) is not A? I make answer: TC as omni-greatness is indeed blemished by evil such that TC is not TC for the reason that opposites function at the existential-only level.

TC

TC QUA EXISTENT   NOT-TC QUA EXISTENT

Here: paradox is to faces; as TC qua identity is to TC qua existent and not-TC qua existent non-same cases; as TC is to TC qua omni-greatness and TC qua evil cases; as TC is to God and Satan cases; as TC is to good and evil cases; as TC is to orthodoxy and apostasy cases. By which games-talk, the distinction is made between TC qua identity and TC qua an identity-face, the opposite identity-face of which is not-TC qua evil. I thus see it that the solution to the ontological problem of evil (a problem of being, of identity) is to see it in atonistic terms as an existential case, not an ontological case.

All such atonistic games-talk bespeaks identity as paradox, as atonement, which games-talk presents in sum as follows.

ATONISM

MONISM, THEISM, GOOD   MONISM, ATHEISM, EVIL

Here: paradox is to faces; as Atonism is to non-same cases of Monism: as identity is to theism-over-atheism as the traditional good and atheism-over-theism as the challenging opposite; as duckrabbit is to duck-over-rabbit and rabbit-over-duck processing faces; as TC qua identity without bias is to non-same existents in continual mutual eclipse.

To end. For Atonism, each identity in the story of the world – every case of A = A – is TC as the Word qua something (or that) than which nothing greater can be conceived, necessarily existing dynamically as two-faced, including as good and evil. Atonistically viewed, the magnitude of TC is such that, without bias, as prerogative, it accords parity of esteem to the opposites, extending to them equal right-to-exist privilege. This is the stuff of identity – as each case in the world story.

The Diary work will next engage in a take-up with the identity of Christ to explore its atonistic sense, and as follows

DAY 7: EVIL

Notes

1. An alternative games-talk to that which sees identity to be TC is that which sees identity to be the algebraic x. Just as such x takes all values positive and negative, or just as it takes all values zero and non-zero (whether positive or negative), so TC out pictures as good and evil. For Atonism, just as the algebraic x loses none of its significance as an identity qua paradox where it presents as negative value, so identity qua TC is not blemished by its existence as evil.

2. Yet another games-talk variant is that where identity is called the Third Man. For Plato and Aristotle, where there are paired opposites called instances of Form, Form is the Third Man. Where such Form and instances are opposites, as further instances of a further Form, that further Form is the Third Man, and so on. For Atonism: identity is to opposites; as TC is to good and evil cases; as Third Man is to non-same existents; as duckrabbit is to duck and rabbit faces. This games-talk bespeaks identity (paradox, atonement) as TC, as Third Man. Where Third Man is given an opposite – its instances – it thereby is not identity but an existent-only. Only where it takes no opposite is Third Man an identity qua TC.

DIARY OF ATONEMENT

DAY 8: CHRIST

Today's Diary work aims to explore – including with rehearsal from earlier Diary work – how the games-talk of a unique Christ fits with Atonism.

The rehearsal with addition is this: duckrabbit is to duck and rabbit faces; as identity is to non-same existents; as Man qua Christ is to Man qua God and Man qua Satan cases; as choice qua free-will is to good and evil cases.

CHRIST

GOD   SATAN

Next to which, as variant games-talk: paradox is to faces; as Lord is to Jesus the One and manifold Incarnation cases (threefold as God + Christ + Satan cases).

LORD

JESUS   INCARNATION

As further variant games-talk: paradox is to faces; as identity is to Jones (say) and triad (body, mind, spirit – body, mind, person) cases.

This variant games-talk presents in the following manner.

IDENTITY

JONES   TRIAD

To end. For Atonism, in terms of religious Christian games-talk, each identity in the story of the world – every case of A = A – is Lord as at once One and Many, Jesus and Incarnation, Jones and threefold make-up. In terms of variant games-talk, every identity is Christ as at once good and evil, God and Satan, godly and ungodly, orthodox and apostate, establishment Man and anti-establishment Man, risen Man and fallen Man, establishment-pedestalized Man and establishment-reviled Man, and so on for all cases of opposites. Accordingly, the unique, historical, Christ is every person and everything in the world story, each as identity qua paradox, qua atonement, each as TC qua Word as something than which nothing greater can be conceived.

From which closing atonistic games-talk the Diary work now will turn to see how Modern and Contemporary Philosophy – from Descartes to Wittgenstein – fits with Atonism, this exploration beginning with Descartes, as follows.

DIARY OF ATONEMENT

DAY 9: DESCARTES

Today's Diary work will investigate how the philosophy of Descartes fits with Atonism.

Introductory comments

1. I see it that games-talk qua Scholasticism – the medieval tradition of thought which sought to reconcile faith and reason (Christian Roman Catholic theology and Aristotelian philosophy) – was contested by Descartes who subjected all received-sense games-talk to a method of radical scepticism, the method of doubt: he fathered a modern philosophy (post-traditional at his day). For medieval games-talk, God is the sole source of truth. For Descartes the philosopher, the human mind (as clear and distinct perceptions qua ideas) is the source of the truth of the existence of God. This Cartesian philosophy I see to be the modern philosophy of Rationalism. By it, knowledge begins with the mind.

2. Too, I see it that, for Descartes, Reason reasons the divine existence as a truth, and God guarantees the veracity of Reason. That is, for Descartes, God creates reason and reason then reasons there to be God as its Creator. (Descartes in effect argues that whatever he distinctly and clearly perceives to exist, thereby truly does so – in this case, God; and that God, as a benevolent non-deceiver, guarantees the truth of the clear and distinct idea. That is: idea, therefore God; God, therefore idea). I understand that this games-talk, as a seemingly circular reasoning of Descartes, is called the case of the Cartesian circle (so see, next comment). Employing what he sees to be clear, distinct, ideas of reason, Descartes' thinking includes offering an Ontological Argument for the existence of God, seen to be perfect being.

3. Further comment on the Cartesian circular reasoning runs out as follows. Its argument is this: what we clearly and distinctly perceive is true only because God exists; but we can be sure God exists only because we clearly and distinctly perceive this.

For Atonism, this Cartesian argument is games-talk which gives voice to a threefold sense of God, viz., God the idea, God the reality, and God as both at once (God the atonement, identity, paradox).

IDENTITY, GOD THE ATONEMENT

EXISTENT, GOD THE IDEA   EXISTENT, GOD THE REALITY

Here: duckrabbit is to duck and rabbit faces; as God the atonement is to God the idea and God the reality existents. From which games-talk, Cartesian circular reasoning instances paradox logic, the logic of identity as atonement.

Atonistic variant games-talk, in Christian terms, is this: God the atonement is to God the idea and God the reality existents: as Lord qua Christ is to God and Satan existents; as Man of freedom is to orthodox, godly, Man (pedestalized qua establishment-applauded) and apostate, ungodly, Man (fallen qua establishment reviled) existents; as person is to idea qua ideal (mind, soul) and real qua material (body) natures. In terms of games-talk of the Blessed Trinity: just as there is God the (begetting) Father, God the (begotten) Son, and God the Holy Spirit; so there is God the idea (God the perfect being), God the reality, and God the atonement (identity, paradox); so – as will be proposed shortly – there is thinking (verb sense), thinking (noun sense), and thinking substance as both at once; and so there is thinking activity, thought content, and mind as both at once. Another variant is this: God the atonement is to God the idea and God the reality existents; as identity is to non-same existents qua the A = A form and any/all content expressing that form. A consequence of this latter games-talk is that Christ as the Son is both Son of God (S.O.G) and Son of Man (S.O.M), that is, the Son is both the eternal S.O.G. in the context of the Blessed Trinity games-talk and the temporal S.O.M. in the context of the Incarnation games-talk. For Atonism, all such games-talk is a variant of the Cartesian games-talk called by the received mind-set the Cartesian circle (= circular reasoning). All such talk bespeaks paradox logic – identity as atonement, as paradox.

The introductory three comments now made, I shall see as itself received-sense games-talk the following Cartesian clear and distinct ideas, as relevant for today's Diary work.

Key features of Cartesian philosophy

- Descartes the doubter, hence the thinker, thinks: cogito ergo sum (I think, therefore I am), by which thinking he discovers himself indubitably to exist.

- Descartes thereby discovers himself qua thinker to exist as indubitably a thinking substance.

- Descartes discovers in his thinking the innate idea of an infinite being and thereby discovers – by the principle that a cause contains at least as much reality as its effect – that an infinite being (God), as the sole possible cause of the idea, indubitably exists as the cause of his innate idea. The argument is this: what we clearly and distinctly perceive is true only because God exists; but we can be sure God exists only because we clearly and distinctly perceive this.

- Descartes discovers that God, as perfect benevolent being who thus would never deceive him as to the real existence of the world and his own body, is indubitably the guarantor of such reality, hence the world, and his body, indubitably exist.

- Descartes finds for the pineal gland – a tiny organ in the centre of the brain – as the main seat of the soul and the location of vital spirits.

The features now given, I move next to ask the question: how does the Cartesian philosophy – its games-talk – fit with Atonism? To treat with this question, I shall again lay out the above key features of the philosophy of Descartes, but this time with associated atonistic presentation and games-talk, as follows.

Cartesian and atonistic games-talk

 Descartes the doubter, hence the thinker, thinks: *cogito ergo sum* (I think, therefore I am), by which thinking he discovers himself indubitably to exist.

 Descartes thereby discovers himself qua thinker to exist as indubitably a thinking substance.

THINKING SUBSTANCE

THINKING (VERB SENSE)   THINKING (NOUN SENSE)

Here: duckrabbit is to duck and rabbit faces; as *ergo* is to *cogito/sum* cases (antecedent/consequent flanking cases); as the I is to mental/extra-mental cases (subjective/objective cases); as thought is to thinking/thinking cases (verb-sense/noun-sense cases). For Atonism, as added games-talk, thinking (verb sense) yields both sure truths and doubts.

THINKING ACTIVITY

TRUTHS   DOUBTS

DAY 9: DESCARTES 45

 Descartes discovers in his thinking the innate idea of an infinite being and thereby discovers – by the principle that a cause contains at least as much reality as its effect – that an infinite being (God), as the sole possible cause of the idea, indubitably exists as the cause of his innate idea. The argument is this: what we clearly and distinctly perceive is true only because God exists; but we can be sure God exists only because we clearly and distinctly perceive this.

IDENTITY, GOD THE ATONEMENT, CAUSATION

EXISTENT,   EXISTENT,
GOD THE IDEA, CAUSE   GOD THE REALITY, EFFECT

Here: duckrabbit is to duck and rabbit faces; as God the causation is to God the caused idea and God the causal reality existents. From which games-talk, Cartesian circular reasoning instances paradox logic, the logic of identity as atonement. For fuller consideration of this Cartesian games-talk, see the Introductory comments section, from earlier.

 Descartes discovers that God, as perfect benevolent being who thus would never deceive him as to the real existence of the world and his own body, is indubitably the guarantor of such reality, hence the world, and his body, indubitably exist.

GOD

IDEAS   REALITY

Here: duckrabbit is to duck and rabbit faces; as God is to ideal (the idea) and real non-same (distinct) existents. By this variant games-talk the principle of causation is God, the faces of which are not now the God-idea and the real-God but are the mind and body non-same existents (ideas and reality, intelligibility and extension, the ideal and the material, the world-idea and the real-world cases) – the opposites operating in tandem, like all opposite cases, in the manner of paradox faces in process of continual mutual eclipse. Again, for fuller treatment of how the word 'God' is to be understood atonistically, see the earlier section of Introductory comments, dealing with what the received mind-set calls the Cartesian circular reasoning.

 Descartes finds for the pineal gland – a tiny organ in the centre of the brain – as the main seat of the soul and the location of vital spirits.

PINEAL GLAND

SOUL (MIND) BODY (MATTER)

Here: duckrabbit is to duck and rabbit faces; as pineal gland is to non-same cases of soul and vital spirits (mind and, say, nerve processes); as location is to located distinct cases; as coincidence is to coincident cases.

In sum, I see it in terms of the foregoing variant games-talk that: pineal gland is to intelligibility (soul) and extension (say, nerves) cases; as thinking substance is to thinking (verb-sense) and thoughts cases; as person is to mind and body existents; as causation is to cause and effect cases; as paradox qua circular reasoning is to God-idea and real-God cases, also to world-idea and real-world cases (where, in the latter case, it is God qua God the atonement, the paradox, playing out as opposites).

DAY 9: DESCARTES

Further to the foregoing assorted language games – each bespeaking identity as atonement, as paradox – there is Cartesian variant games-talk, untreated in detail until now, of an evil demon intent upon inspiring the Cartesian mind with doubt. The *cogito* argument ('I think, therefore I am') is devised by Descartes to put paid to all doubt and vanquish the demon.

KNOWLEDGE

GOD, SURENESS   DEMON, DOUBT

Here: duckrabbit is to duck and rabbit faces; as knowledge is to the cases of what-is and what-is-not opposites; as eclipse is to eclipsing surety (personified as a good qua benevolent God) and eclipsed doubt (personified as an evil qua malignant demon). By this games-talk I see it that Cartesian Monism qua Rationalism (championing oneness qua consistency-sense as the criterion of rationality) is given the ascendancy over doubt (doubt qua all pre-Cartesian received-sense thinking as, now, doubted thinking), in the manner in which the duckrabbit is seen fixedly as one-only of its faces, in repression of its other face.

A wider view

Drawing not only on today's Diary work but also on that of previous days, assorted games-talk runs out as follows. This wider view rehearses with addition the section from earlier, viz., Introductory comments.

TC is to paired opposites; as duckrabbit is to duck and rabbit faces; as experience is to good and evil existents; as Lord is to God and Satan existents; as Cartesian critical Man is to good, orthodox, Man and evil, apostate, Man existents; as free-will Man is to establishment-Man and anti-establishment Man existents.

More: TC is to paired opposites; as Man writ large as Christ the Lord is to pro-Christ godly (orthodox) Man writ large as God and anti-Christ ungodly (apostate)

Man writ large as Satan; as Christian Lord is to transcendent (pedestalized) God and transcended (Fallen) Man; as the Cartesian modern philosophy is to the Cartesian Jesuit conditioned mind-set of absolute conviction and the Cartesian evil demon mind-set of absolute scepticism; as atonement is to distinct cases of divine truth-ground and demonic temptation to doubt.

Too, TC is to paired opposites; as Atonism is to the opposite cases of medieval Catholic Monism (giving ascendancy to God, the One, over fallen human reason, also to Jesus as the sole Christ) and Monism qua Materialism (championing each one of the Many, in rejection of Monism qua the One); as Atonism is to Rationalism (giving ascendancy to Reason – mind, soul, the One – over manifold body) and Empiricism identity-faces.

These assorted language games present in the following manner.

TC, IDENTITY, PARADOX
LORD
MAN AS CHRIST
ATONISM

EXISTENT CASES QUA PARADOX FACES
IN CONTINUAL MUTUAL ECLIPSE

GOD	SATAN
ORTHODOX MAN	APOSTATE MAN
GOOD GOD	EVIL DEMON
MEDIEVAL CATHOLIC MONISM	MONISM QUA MATERIALISM
RATIONALISM	EPIRICISM

Conclusion

By proposal, Rationalism gives the ascendancy to Reason over each of the Revelation and Materialism opposite cases yet shares with them in championing singularity-as-singleness-sense to be the stuff of identity, hence consistency as the criterion of rationality. For Atonism, the Cartesian modern philosophy as Monism qua Rationalism puts out an epistemology (that all knowledge starts with the mind) which is opposite to that of Monism qua Empiricism (all knowledge is a function of sense data, each datum as a oneness). Accordingly, for Atonism, Rationalism is a face-only of identity, an opposite face being Empiricism. By which atonistic perspective, each identity in the story of the world – every case of A = A – as TC qua the Word, as that than which nothing greater can be conceived, is rational as paradoxically empirical, divine as paradoxically mundane, good as paradoxically evil, and so on for all cases of opposites as faces of paradox, identity, atonement qua atoncement.

I next turn to an atonistic study of Empiricism, as put out by Hume.

Notes

1. I see it that Descartes equates identity and existence as well as opposes mental nature (the concept) and extra-mental nature (the reality). In his Ontological Argument for the existence of God he reasons that God, as in concept perfection, which perfection by intuition includes necessary existence, thereby is a necessarily real existent – God in concept = God identity as a reality, viz., an existent. For Atonism, however, the games-talk is this: duckrabbit is to duck and rabbit faces; as identity is to distinct existents (together making for existence qua ex-istence, as out-pictures); as Lord is to God and Satan cases; as Cartesian Man is to orthodox Man and apostate Man; as identity qua TC (which Descartes calls God, as perfection) is to conceptual and real existents; as God the atonement is to God the ideal and God the real existents. An alternative games-talk bespeaks the Cartesian idea not as a concept but as an intuition, or form, as a Platonic Idea – a direct vision as neither intellectual nor physical in kind. By it, one 'just sees', for example, that 2 and 2 make 4, or that to think is to exist, or to be perfect is to necessarily be.

2. It is interesting to see the Cartesian pineal gland as the pictorializing, as it were, of the Cartesian thinking substance.

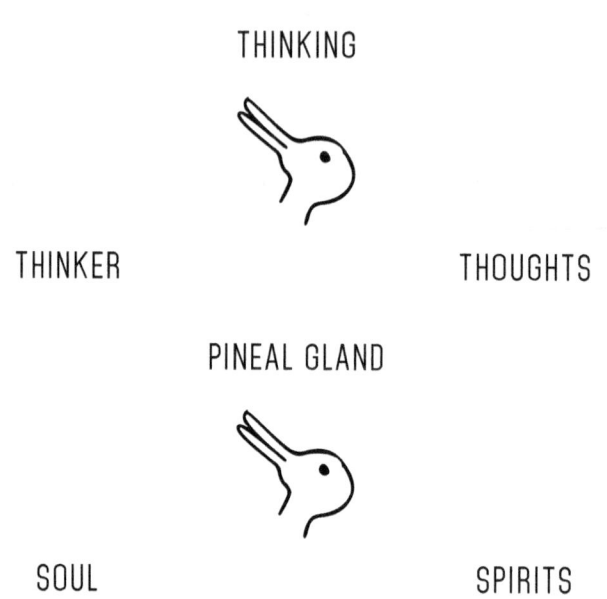

Here: duckrabbit is to duck and rabbit faces; as thinking substance is to thinking (verb sense) and thinking (noun sense) cases; as thinking *per se* is to thinker and thought content (body of thoughts) cases; as pineal gland qua meeting place is to soul (mind) and spirits (thoughts) cases.

Other assorted language games are as follows.

DAY 9: DESCARTES 51

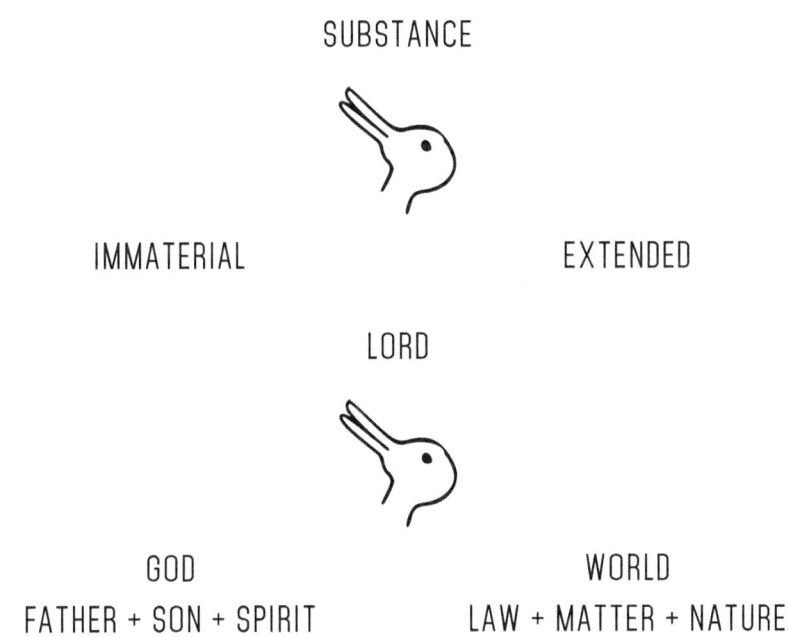

SUBSTANCE

IMMATERIAL EXTENDED

LORD

GOD WORLD
FATHER + SON + SPIRIT LAW + MATTER + NATURE

Here: duckrabbit is to duck and rabbit faces; as (in Catholic doctrine) Spirit is to Father and Son; as substance *per se* is to immaterial substance and extended substance; as (in religious cosmological terms) Lord is to the threefold God (Father + Spirit + Son) and the threefold World (natural law + Nature + matter); as (Lord is to the threefold God (Father + Spirit + Son) and the threefold Man (mind + spirit qua person + body); as Atonism is to Monism and Pluralism.

IDENTITY, DIVINE WILL, PERSON

ACTIVE PRINCIPLE PASSIVE PRINCIPLE

Here: duckrabbit is to duck and rabbit faces; as divine will is to intelligible and sensible cases; as person is to soul and immaterial body (of thoughts cases); as person is to mind and extended body (of behaviours) natures; as (in mixed games talk) person is to soul and physical body existents; as (in mixed games talk) person is to mind and immaterial body (of thoughts) existents; as identity is to active principle (soul, mind) and passive principle (body, immaterial or extended) existents.

By this games talk, since, for Atonism, soul and body (like mind and body) are faces of paradox, the soul survives or exists separately from the body only in the sense in which a face of paradox qua face is distinct from the opposite face qua face. Hence, though distinct as thereby independent cases, the two are (by the logic of paradox) necessarily, hence ever temporally, at once the case – the case of identity as atonement, as paradox, called 'person'.

DIARY OF ATONEMENT

DAY 10: HUME

The objective of the Diary work for today will be to understand Hume's philosophy in atonistic terms, to see how its games-talk fits with Atonism.

By proposal, received-sense language games qua key features of the Humean philosophy – together with their atonistic presentation and games-talk – tell out as follows.

 Hume champions Empiricism, the philosophy that all knowledge results from experience, from sensation (sense data): it is thus knowledge received neither from God nor from innate ideas. It comprises perceptions of two kinds: the impression and its corresponding copy qua idea. Knowledge (perception) is a function not of intuition or faith but of direct observation: there neither is God, nor the innate idea, other than by mere assumption.

EMPIRICAL KNOWLEDGE (PERCEPTION),
DIRECT OBSERVATION, EXPERIENCE

IDEA QUA COPY   IMPRESSION, SENSE DATA

ASSUMPTION

| FAITH | INTUITION |
| GOD | INNATE IDEAS |

Here: paradox is to faces; as identity is to existents; as atonement is to distinct cases; as perception is to impression/idea cases; as assumption is to faith/intuition cases; as assumption is to cases of God and innate ideas.

Except by assumption, there is no causality, no necessary connection between the two events but only a directly observable constant conjunction of events, believed by force of habit as a part of human nature to be a cause-and-effect necessary nexus.

DIRECT OBSERVATION

CONSTANTLY CONJOINED EVENTS

NATURAL HABITUAL BELIEF

CAUSE AND EFFECT NECESSARY NEXUS

DAY 10: HUME

Here: paradox is to faces; as direct observation is to constantly conjoined events; as natural habitual belief is to is to necessarily connected cause and effect cases.

 Other than by mere assumption, there is no principle of induction – no principle that the future is predictable, given the past (for example, no sureness that the sun will rise tomorrow as on all previous days).

ASSUMPTION, PRINCIPLE OF INDUCTION

PAST AND FUTURE PROBABLE CONNECTED CASES

PREVIOUS SUNRISE   FUTURE SUNRISE

Here: paradox is to faces; as atonement is to distinct cases; as assumed principle of induction is to probably connected past and future events (cf. the previous games-talk of natural habitual belief as necessarily connected cause and effect cases).

 Concerning morality, this is entirely utilitarian and is a function of sentiment only: some principles simply appeal to us and others do not according to whether or not they promote our interests and those of our fellow human beings, with whom we naturally sympathize – we simply are biologically inclined to approve and support whatever helps society, since we all live in a community and stand to benefit.

MORALITY

UTILITARIAN SENTIMENTS
BIOLOGICAL BEHAVIOURS

APPROVAL/   CENSURE/
PLEASURE SEEKING   PAIN AVOIDANCE

Here: paradox is to faces; as morality is to diverse utilitarian connected sentiments qua opposite biological behaviours (seeking approval, avoiding censure; seeking pleasure, avoiding pain).

It is solely by mere assumption that morality roots in God's will (authority). Morality is to suit Man, not God. For *Hume's Treatise on Human Nature*, morality is sprung entirely from passion – not from either divine will or human reason – and which passion is common to all humans as part of their nature.

PASSION

MORAL EXPERIENCES

Here: paradox is to faces; as passion is to moral experiences; as assumption is to morality rooted in divine will and morality grounded in innate ideas of human reason – these non-same cases as assumed sources of morality.

ASSUMPTION

DIVINE AND RATIONAL SOURCES OF MORALITY

 There is no such thing as substance, no such entity as the self, or the soul. The reality of such things is nothing other than as a function of natural belief. Substance – say, the self, or the soul – is simply experience of sense-data – impressions, a bundle of perceptions.

CREDULITY

SUBSTANTIAL EXISTENTS

SINGULAR SELF   SINGULAR SOUL

SUBSTANCE, SELF, SOUL, BUNDLE

NON-SAME PERCEPTIONS

Here: paradox is to faces; as credulity is to singular-self and singular-soul substantial existents; as substance (self, soul, bundle) is to bundled non-same perceptions.

On miracles, there are none – other than as a result of human credulity. Laws of nature are universal and uniform, admitting of no exceptions, no violations: experience rules against miracles.

HUMAN CREDULITY

GOD   MIRACLES

Here: paradox is to faces; as credulity is to God and miracle existents.

 On God, there is at best a deity indifferent to good and evil happenings in the world. For given the God of theism – a God involving in the world – the existence of such God would preclude the existence of evil, yet evil exists.

INDIFFERENT DEITY

GOOD   EVIL

Here: paradox is to faces; as indifferent deity is to good and evil happenings.

This completes the presentation of Humean and atonistic games-talk.

General comment

I see it that whether the games-talk be (say) that whereby perception is sense-datum impression and corresponding idea as its copy, or be (say) that whereby credulity alone warrants the causality principle as genuinely epistemological, it

DAY 10: HUME

is a games-talk of identity as atonement, as paradox. This says that Humean games-talk, like the non-Humean games-talk contested by Hume, is a received-sense games-talk which nonetheless lends itself to atonistic analysis.

In wider perspective, I see the differences between empirical Monism and either theistic Monism or rationalist Monism to be these. For theistic Monism, there is the One qua God. For rationalist Monism, there is the One qua Mind (innate Reason). For empirical Monism, there is One qua the perception. But whereas the rationalist Mind, like the God of theism, is the universal One, the empirical perception as the One is but one of Many (Many perceptions). I shall distinguish between the universal One and the particular One by calling the first games-talk macroMonism (say, Theism, Rationalism) and the second games-talk microMonism (say, Empiricism). Atonistic games-talk presents as follows.

ATONISM

MACROMONISM   MICROMONISM

ATONISM

MONISMA QUA RATIONALISM   MONISM QUA EMPIRICISM

ATONISM

MONISM QUA THEISM   MONISM QUA EMPIRICISM

More, I see it that although the cases of Monism, each as not another, are atonistic existents, each, in terms of itself, is an atonistic identity: paradox is to faces; as God is to divine works; as Mind activity is to thoughts; as perception is to impression/idea opposites.

IDENTITY, GOD, MIND, PERCEPTION

EXISTENTS, DIVINE WORKS, THOUGHTS,
IMPRESSION/COPY OPPOSITES

This leaves the following as a problem for Hume: if there is no universal One but only the particular One, how are the particular cases (of perceptions) to be called the one bundle? How can Empiricism qua microMonism be the case?

As this study sees it, a nerve centre of Hume's position is what he cannot say rather than all that he can, and does, say. This that he cannot say is indicated by him in the Appendix to his work A Treatise of Human Nature. There, he states that in sum there are two principles, which he can neither render consistent nor neither of which is he able to renounce. The two principles are these: that all human distinct perceptions are distinct existents, and that the mind is never able to perceive any real connection among such distinct existents.

I see it by this games-talk of Hume that there are distinct perceptions without any discernible (by the mind) real connection, leaving it that the case of a collection (the existents) as nothing collected (no connecting activity) makes for inconsistency, defeating (he thinks) his Empiricism as an effective philosophy of Monism (oneness sense, consistency). Each existent qua each perception, in terms of the others, is a consistency (oneness sense). But without any connectedness among the existents (the distinct perceptions) there is no (discernible) overall consistency (oneness sense). It is for this reason that Hume sees his Empiricism to be defective. It does not, for him, suffice as a philosophy of Monism – Monism which champions consistency as

DAY 10: HUME

the criterion of rationality (reality, identity, being). This leaves Hume in scepticism re: his empirical philosophy. There is (for him) no known reality called identity (overall oneness, unity) though this flies in the face of common-sense experience.

For Atonism, distinct existents (perceptions or any others) indeed are not in any way connected for they are simply at once the case, the case thereby of atonement (identity, paradox). This explains why no connectedness among distinct case is discernible. The distinct existents are the faces of paradox (the duck is in no way a rabbit, nor vice versa). Understandably, a collection as nothing collected is for Monism – Monism championing consistency qua oneness-sense as the criterion of rationality, hence of reality (identity, being) – a case of contradiction, a case of nonsense. For Atonism however, contradiction (nonsense) is not the case and neither is consistency (Monism, oneness sense) the case. Rather, Atonism is the case, the case of identity qua paradox as the atonement of distinct-existents qua faces of paradox.

The games-talk presents as follows.

IDENTITY

EXISTENTS

ATONEMENT, NO CONNECTIVITY

DISTINCT EXISTENTS (PERCEPTIONS)

Here: paradox is to faces; as non-connectivity is to distinct cases; as atonement is to opposite cases; as identity is to non-same existents; as Atonism is to non-same cases of Monism (non-same cases of oneness). For Atonism, nothing whatever connects paradox-faces; they simply are at once the case, the case thereby of atonement, the case of identity (paradox) as opposites.

Conclusion

Atonistically understood, the thinking of Hume as games-talk bespeaks each identity in the story of the world – every case of A = A – as atonistic identity, TC, the Word qua something (or that) than which nothing greater can be conceived. Here (drawing from all Diary work up to now), a mixed games-talk is this: each identity is paradoxically rational and empirical, innate idea and sense impression, ideated copies and sense data, mind-natured and body-natured, idealistic and earthy, good and evil, godly and ungodly, God and Satan, orthodox Man and apostate Man, establishment-applauded Man and establishment-reviled Man, pedestalized Man and fallen Man, and so on for all opposite cases, cases as faces of identity as paradox, as atonement qua atoncement.

The philosophies of Rationalism and Empiricism now having been treated with atonistically, the Diary work next turns to treat atonistically with the critical philosophy of Kant, as follows.

DIARY OF ATONEMENT

DAY 11: KANT

The Diary work for today will investigate the philosophy of Kant to discover in what ways certain of its many different aspects fit with Atonism. The selected aspects to be targeted are these: (1) Kant on scientific knowledge; (2) Kant on morality and religion.

Initial comments

First, I see it that Kant is critical of both Rationalism as put out by Descartes and Empiricism as put out by Hume. Accordingly, Kant's is a critical philosophy which rejects the thesis that knowledge begins with the mind (its ideas as innate ideas) as well as rejects the thesis that knowledge begins with sense impressions. Rather, for Kant, knowledge arises from the interrelationship between mind and the senses, though not in terms of mind qua ideas as innate.

CRITICAL PHILOSOPHY, INTERRELATIONSHIPS

RATIONALISM   EMPIRICISM

Here: duckrabbit is to duck and rabbit paradox-faces; as identity is to distinct existents; as Kantian critical philosophy is to Rationalism and Empiricism non-same philosophies; as interrelationship is to interrelated distinct cases.

Second, I see the Kantian games-talk to present as a philosophy which puts out with great intricacy of meaning, using considerable technical terminology.

For these reasons, rather than using bullet points to list proposed salient features of the Kantian talk, I shall make use from the outset of economy, also of Kantian vocabulary blended with my own language as interpretive of that vocabulary, together with atonistic games-talk attended by its pictorial presentations – all as follows.

(1) *Kant on scientific knowledge*

Our senses, affected by external objects, provide sensory matter, shaped (= formed, ordered) by the intuitive mind to yield immediate perception of objects as phenomena qua appearances in space and time. Here, mind and matter (form and sensation) correspond. The objects qua space-time content are at the same time formed (= conceptualized qua categorized) by the discursive mind to be understood as objects of (say) substance, quantity and quality. This experience of (co-operative intuition and thought) objects constitutes scientific knowledge. Here, mind and content (form and content) correspond.

CORRESPONDENCE. ORDER

INTUITIVE   SPACE-TIME
ORDERING MIND   ORDERED DATA

CORRESPONDENCE. ORDER

DISCURSIVE   CONCEPTUALLY
ORDERING MIND   ORDERED DATA

DAY 11: KANT

SCIENTIFIC KNOWLEDGE, CO-OPERATION

THOUGHT   INTUITION

Here: duckrabbit is to duck and rabbit paradox-faces; as identity is to distinct existents; as correspondence is to corresponding cases; as appearance is to intuitive mind and intuited sense data cases; as order is to form and matter cases; as understanding is to discursive mind and categorized space-time cases; as order is to form and content cases; as co-operation is to co-operating cases; as scientific knowledge is to thought and intuition cases.

Correlative with human knowledge phenomenon is the noumenon (= the unknowable), something posited by Kant to be that which affects our senses, triggering the process of scientific knowledge acquisition. The noumenon (plural: noumena), also referred to by Kant as the thing-in-itself (in contrast with the thing-in-appearance), is also called the transcendental object (= that which transcends qua lies outside human knowledge).

CORRELATION

NOUMENON   PHENOMENON

Here: duckrabbit is to duck and rabbit paradox-faces; as identity is to distinct existents; as atonement is to opposite cases; as correlation is to noumenon and phenomenon correlated cases.

The objects of scientific knowledge are necessarily and universally what they are, viz., space-time categorized objects, since the intuitive and discursive faculties of mind, by their very nature, so shape them, albeit that the objects also are of sense-data origin. This leaves it that scientific knowledge is knowledge said by Kant to be synthetic *a priori* – synthetic meaning of sensory origin and *a priori* meaning of transcendental qua universal necessary character – transcendental meaning beyond qua distinct from anything that is *a posteriori* (= deriving from sensory experience).

SYNTHETIC A PRIORI

OF SENSIBLE ORIGIN   UNIVERSAL NECESSITY

Here: duckrabbit is to duck and rabbit paradox-faces; as identity is to distinct existents; as atonement is to opposite cases; as synthetic *a priori* is to the tied-together cases of that which is of sensible origin and that which is of necessary universality.

(2) *Kant on morality and religion*

In addition to the use of pure reason to do with *a priori* principles such as those featuring in the acquisition of scientific knowledge, there is practical reason to do with the performance of actions, notably those relating to moral behaviour, and involving religious faith.

HUMAN EXPERIENCE

SCIENTIFIC KNOWLEDGE   RELIGIOUS MORALITY

Here: duckrabbit is to duck and rabbit paradox-faces; as identity is to distinct existents; as human experience is to the cases of scientific knowledge and morality which postulates the existence of God.

DAY 11: KANT

Kant holds that the pure reason which gives out in *a priori* principles also gives out in these three ideas: God, freedom, and immortality. These are ideas the reality of which pure reason cannot prove. It is for practical reason (connected with morality) that these ideas are importantly significant.

PURE REASON

IDEAS OF GOD, FUTURE LIFE, FREEDOM

Here: duckrabbit is to duck and rabbit paradox-faces; as identity is to distinct existents; as pure reason is to non-same ideas, each not another (God, future life of soul, freedom).

The Kantian argument is that moral law demands justice, viz., happiness proportional to virtue. Since this is not humanly achievable in this life there is need for three postulates which together render justice achievable: the existence of God (guarantor of such justice); the existence of hereafter (wherein the soul achieves such justice); and the existence of freedom (since virtue implies free will). For Kant, morality consists in obedience to the dictate of pure reason (in its practical aspect and felt as conscience) speaking the necessary Categorical Imperative to act only on that maxim willed as universal law.

PRACTICAL REASON, JUSTICE

VIRTUE　　　　　　　　HAPPINESS

POSTULATES: GOD, FUTURE LIFE, FREEDOM

Here: duckrabbit is to duck and rabbit paradox-faces; as justice is to virtue and happiness cases; as justice is to postulates, each not another (God, future life of soul, freedom).

MORALITY

CATEGORICAL IMPERATIVE   MORAL CONDUCT

Here: duckrabbit is to duck and rabbit paradox-faces; as morality is to categorical imperative and moral conduct cases.

In this sense of justice requiring postulates, including the postulate re: the existence of God, Kant rejects proofs of pure reason for divine existence to make room for faith.

ECLIPSE

REASON   FAITH

Here: duckrabbit is to duck and rabbit paradox-faces; as eclipse is to eclipsing-faith and eclipsed reason cases.

Assessment

For Atonism, whether the Kantian games-talk speaks in terms of interrelationship (of Rationalism and Empiricism), correspondence (of mind and data), co-operation (of thought and intuition), correlation (of noumenon and phenomenon, synthetic *a priori* (= universal necessity and sensible origin), human experience (of scientific knowledge and religious morality), pure reason (as ideas), practical reason (as postulates); justice (as virtue and happiness), morality (as imperative and conduct), or eclipse (as faith over reason), it is games-talk of identity as distinct existents, atonement as opposite cases, paradox as its faces.

I see it that Kant's thinking is that of Monism which champions consistency as the criterion of rationality (reality, being, identity). The opposites I see to be non-same cases of Monism (one-ism) whether talk be of the One over the Many (critical philosophy over other philosophies, ordering mind over the ordered manifold qua Many ones) or each one of the Many.

Too – as variant games-talk – there is Monism in its religious attire as Monotheism as the talk of one faith in one God. More, where – as variant games-talk – correlation of noumenon and phenomenon cases is seen to be talk of Christ as divine and mundane cases, there is Monism in its religious attire of Christian Monotheism as the talk of one correlation (reconciliation cf. the Atonement) as one Christ.

From previous Diary work, this is Christ as at once pro-Christ and anti-Christ – good and evil, God and Satan, godly and ungodly, orthodoxy and apostasy, establishment-applauded Man and establishment-reviled Man. Kant's talk of virtue is talk of eclipse (good over evil, the One over each one of the Many, God the guarantor of justice over humans unable to achieve happiness as at once virtue).

Conclusion

For Atonism, the thinking of Kant as games-talk bespeaks each identity in the story of the world – every case of A = A – as atonistic identity, TC, the Word qua something (or that) than which nothing greater can be conceived. Bringing together thought and sensibility as the case of human knowledge, Kant in effect brings together the natures of mind and body as the person. In bringing together the good God and human beings unable to achieve virtue with happiness as justice, Kant in effect brings together good and evil as religious morality. In bringing together the noumenal and the phenomenal as a correlation, Kant in effect brings together God and Satan as Christ. Accordingly, I see it that, whether in terms of knowledge, morality, or religion, Kant brings together opposites as at once the case, the case of identity as atonement, as paradox – the case of each identity in the world story putting out as assorted language games.

Moving on, now, from Cartesian, Humean, and Kantian games-talk of the Modern era, we next shall treat with a fourth games-talk from this era, viz., that voiced by Hegel, as follows.

DIARY OF ATONEMENT

DAY 12: HEGEL

Today's Diary work will explore how Hegelian philosophy fits with the thought form of Atonism.

I see it that Hegel's philosophy conceptualizes the Christian story (Christian Monotheism pictures Hegelian Monism). Hence, received scholarship notwithstanding, I see there to be the following traditional games-talk equivalents (Christian and Hegelian). These I set out, first in a brief version, followed by an expanded version.

The games: brief version

- Christ consciousness = Spirit = Totality = Actuality
- God = Absolute = Subjective Spirit = Whole = One
- Man = World = Objective Spirit = Nature = One
- Christ = God + Man (World)
- Actuality = actualizing + actualized
- God = Father + Son + Holy Spirit
- Absolute = ideating + ideated + Idea
- Absolute = reasoning + reasoned + Reason
- Absolute = thinking + thoughts + Thought
- World = realizing + realized + Reality

World = organizing + organized + Organism

 Man = mind + body + person

The games: expanded version

First, I shall take Hegel's games-talk of Spirit to be talk of it as existing both subjectively, as Subjective Spirit, and objectively, as Objective Spirit.

SPIRIT

SUBJECTIVE SPIRIT　　　　OBJECTIVE SPIRIT

Here: duckrabbit is to duck and rabbit faces; as identity is to distinct existents; as Spirit *per se* is to Subjective Spirit + Objective Spirit cases.

Next, I shall take Spirit to mean Consciousness.

CONSCIOUSNESS

SUBJECTIVE CONSCIOUSNESS　　　OBJECTIVE CONSCIOUSNESS

Here: paradox is to faces; as Consciousness *per se* is to Subjective Consciousness + Objective Consciousness cases.

Next, I see Spirit to exist, for example, as both Hegel's philosophy and the Christian story.

DAY 12: HEGEL

SPIRIT

HEGEL, PHILOSOPHY   CHRISTIANITY, STORY

Here: paradox is to faces; as Spirit is to the spirit of Hegel's philosophy + the spirit of the Christian story cases.

Next, I see variant games-talk to say this: Spirit *per se* is the Totality; Subjective Spirit is the Absolute qua Whole; and Objective Spirit is World qua Nature.

THE TOTALITY

THE ABSOLUTE QUA WHOLE   THE WORLD QUA NATURE

Here: paradox is to faces; as the Totality is to the Absolute qua Whole + the World qua Nature cases.

Next, I see it that Spirit *per se* is in variant terms called Christ as both God and Man.

CHRIST

GOD   MAN

Here: paradox is to faces; as Christ is to God + Man cases.

Next, I see it that another variant is that which bespeaks Spirit *per se* as Actuality, and this as the actualizing Spirit of the actualized Spirit.

ACTUALITY

ACTUALIZING   ACTUALIZED

Here: paradox is to faces; as Actuality (Spirit, Christ, the Totality) is to actualizing + actualized cases.

Next, I see there to be the three orders of Monism: the Totality qua One (Christ); the Absolute qua One (God), and the World qua One (Man).

MONISM: THE TOTAL ONE

MONISM: THE ABSOLUTE ONE   MONISM: THE WORLD ONE

Here: paradox is to faces; as Monism qua the Total One is to Monism qua the Absolute One + Monism qua the World One (universe) cases.

Next, regarding each of the opposites, each as One, I see it to be itself Many (ones) as a threefold games-talk, again as variant games-talk of that bespeaking Spirit *per se* as Spirit agency + Spirit outcome cases. This clarifies as follows.

Of God, there is the Trinity, viz., the Holy Spirit as the begetting Father + the begotten Son.

DAY 12: HEGEL

HOLY SPIRIT

FATHER   SON

Here: paradox is to its faces; as duckrabbit is to duck and rabbit faces; as identity is to distinct existents; as (re: God) Holy Spirit is to the begetting Father + the begotten Son cases. The talk is of Many qua Trinity as threefold Monism (three Persons): one identity as paradox (Holy Spirit) as one existent (Father) + one non-same existent (Son).

Next, regarding the Absolute, I see the triad (threefold Monism): Idea as opposite cases, viz., the ideating of the ideated cases. In variant games-talk terms, I see this to be the triad (threefold Monism): Reason as opposite cases, viz., the reasoning of the reasoned cases, also Thought as opposite cases, viz., the thinking of itself cases (Thought as the thinking of thoughts cases).

IDEA, REASON, THOUGHT

IDEATING, REASONING,   IDEATED, REASONED,
THINKING   THOUGHTS

Here: paradox is to its faces; as (re: the Absolute Whole) Idea is to ideating + ideated cases; as Reason is to reasoning + reasoned cases; as Thought is to Thinking + itself cases; as Thought is to thinking + thoughts cases; as Monism (one paradox) is to non-same cases of Monism.

Next, regarding the World: Reality is the realizing of the realized cases. As variant: Organism (or Organization) is the organizing of the organized cases.

REALITY, ORGANISM

REALIZING, ORGANIZING   REALIZED, ORGANIZED

Here: paradox is to faces; as (re: the manifold World) Reality is to realizing + realized cases; as Organism (or Organization) is to organizing + organized cases; as Monism (one paradox) is to non-same cases of Monism.

Next, regarding the human World – Man.

PERSON

MIND   BODY

Here: paradox is to faces; as (re: Man) person is to mind(ing) + body cases; as Monism (one paradox) is to non-same cases of Monism.

Next, as variant Hegelian games-talk in mixed-talk terms, I see the Total One to be as rational as it is real. This says that the Total One is Reason as Reality and Reality as Reason.

DAY 12: HEGEL

THE TOTAL ONE

REASON REALITY

Here: paradox is to faces; as the Total One is to Reason + Reality cases; as Monism (one paradox) is to non-same cases of Monism.

Next, I see it that Hegel puts out games-talk of Lord-and-Bondsman (Master-and-Slave) interdependence between persons, or between natures. I see this to be games-talk of the eclipsing-and-eclipsed faces of paradox, faces of identity (individual or social). This talk says that Spirit *per se* is a logic of paradox – by that logic, its faces necessarily process in continual mutual eclipse.

INTERDEPENDENCE, ECLIPSE

LORD, MASTER, ECLIPSING FACE   BONDSMAN, SLAVE, ECLIPSED FACE

Here: paradox is to faces; as interdependence is to Lord + Bondsman (Master and Slave) cases; as eclipse is to eclipsing + eclipsed faces; as Monism (one paradox) is to non-same cases of Monism; as paradox is to mutually eclipsing faces.

Whatever the games-talk variant, I see it to bespeak a triadic dialectic process, abbreviated as TDP. This sense I shall take to mean the logic of paradox whereby – to rehearse – opposite cases qua paradox faces necessarily process in continual mutual eclipse. The TDP I see to be signed by the identity equation $A = A$ wherein the cases of A, as non-same terms and in this sense opposites, continually pass over into one another as moments of identity as their coincidence, signed by =. The moments I see to be paradox faces and the identity I see to be their atonement as the paradox.

=

A   A

Here: paradox is to its faces; as identity is to non-same existents; as identity (signed in A = A by =) is to A/A cases.

I see TDP to be captured by the Hegel games-talk of Becoming as the case of the opposites: Being + Nothing. I see this to bespeak identity as paradox, called Becoming, the faces of which – by reason of paradox logic – necessarily process in continual mutual eclipse, each ever coming to be (as Being) and ceasing to be (as Nothing). This presents as the following atonistic games-talk.

BECOMING
PARADOX

BEING   NOTHING
COMING TO BE   CEASING TO BE

Here: duckrabbit is to duck and rabbit faces; as identity is to distinct existents; as Becoming is to Being + Nothing cases; as paradox is to faces ever coming to be and ceasing to be; as Monism (one paradox) is to non-same cases of Monism.

This concludes the expanded version presentation. Such is my understanding of Hegelian games-talk as a variant of the games-talk of Christian Monotheism, viz., one identity as paradox (Christ) = one existent (God) + one non-same existent (Man, World).

I now move to offer added games-talk, as follows.

Three further comments

First (to rehearse from earlier, with addition), I see it that Hegelian games-talk voices Spirit as both philosophy and Christian story and does so, notably, in terms of history: just as Christian Monotheism speaks of there being but one historical Christ, so Hegel's Monism speaks of there being but the one Totality as historical process.

SPIRIT

HEGELIAN HISTORICAL PROCESS   CHRISTIAN HISTORICAL STORY

Here, in rehearsal: duckrabbit is to duck and rabbit faces; as identity is to distinct existents; as Spirit is to the Hegelian historical process + the Christian story cases; as Monism (one paradox) is to non-same cases of Monism (paradox faces).

Second, I take Hegelian games-talk to be that of Idealism to do with the Absolute qua One, the opposite games-talk being Materialism to do with the World qua One. In variant terms, Hegel's games-talk is that of Rationalism, its opposite being that of Empiricism. For although Reason is Reality and Reality is Reason, the Idea actualizes in history. I see this to imply Dualism: cause prior to effect; Reason over Reality, God over Man, the ideal over the gross, form over matter, and so on.

SPIRIT, ECLIPSE

REASON ECLIPSES REALITY   REALITY ECLIPSED BY REASON

Here, in rehearsal: duckrabbit is to duck and rabbit faces; as identity is to distinct existents; as Spirit is to the eclipsing Reason + eclipsed Reality cases; as Atonism is to Idealism + Materialism cases.

Third, I see it that Hegel's games-talk stops short at the Totality.

ATONISM, TC, LORD

JESUS, ONE   INCARNATION

THE TOTALITY, CHRIST, ONE PARADOX

TOTALLED ONES: ABSOLUTE + WORLD, GOD + MAN

Here, in rehearsal: duckrabbit is to duck and rabbit faces; as identity is to distinct existents; as Atonism is to Monism (Jesus) + threefold Monism (Incarnation) cases.

From which third-comment talk, Hegelian games-talk, conceptualizing orthodox Christian games-talk, tells out that there is but one Totality, one-

DAY 12: HEGEL 81

only Christ, one-only case of identity as paradox, and which Hegelian games-talk, for this reason, I see to be traditional Monism conceptualizing Christian Monotheism.

True, 'Monotheism' means 'one-only God' but I take Christian Monotheism to mean one-only Christ as one-only God manifesting in one-only World personalized as Man (one-only humankind). Hegelian games-talk, seen atonistically, grounds in Monism. To recall the 'Third Man' games-talk given out in the Diary entry on Evil, TC and faces (Lord case and Jesus/Incarnation cases) has no Third Man whereas the Hegelian Totality case and totalled cases does have a Third Man (so see the above diagrammatic presentation.

Even so, I see it that the above presentation is that of assorted language games, each bespeaking identity as paradox, as atonement.

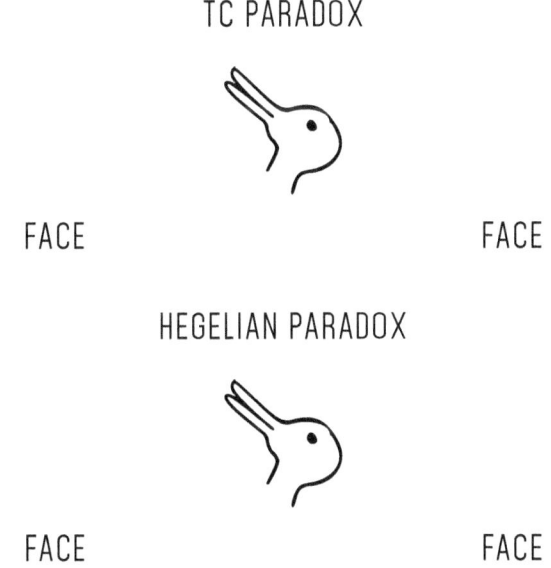

Here, in rehearsal: duckrabbit is to duck and rabbit faces; as identity is to distinct existents; as Atonism qua TC is to paradox faces; as Atonism qua Hegelian paradox is to paradox faces. This says that whereas Hegel's games-talk (conceptualizing Christian orthodox games-talk) finds for a closed system, so to speak, atonistic games-talk finds for opposites such that whatever is closed is paradoxically open: orthodoxy is paradoxically apostasy; Hegelian philosophy is paradoxically any other non-Hegelian philosophy.

An implication is this: whereas Hegelian philosophy, like Christian orthodoxy, champions good over evil, Atonism countenances good and evil being paradoxically one another.

I now turn to this case of good and evil, as follows.

Good and evil

For the work of this section I draw on previous-entry Diary work, relating this, now, to Hegelian games-talk seen as the conceptual variant of Christian games-talk.

I see it that Christian games-talk bespeaks a transcendent God over a fallen (transcended) human world. I take this games-talk to signify the sense (knowledge) of good over evil. I see this, in Hegelian games-talk terms, to be the case of the Absolute Whole over the natural World.

Here: paradox is to faces; as identity is to One over Many existent cases; as Totality is to Absolute over World cases; as Christ is to God over Man cases; as knowledge is to good over evil cases.

Too, I see variant games-talk to present in the following manner.

DAY 12: HEGEL

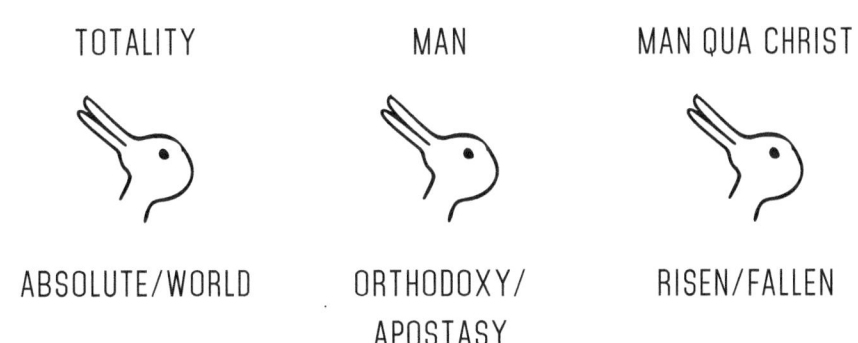

Here: paradox is to faces; as Totality is to Absolute Whole + natural World cases; as Man is to orthodoxy + apostasy cases; as Man is to establishment-pedestalized Man + establishment-reviled Man; as Man qua Christ is to risen (raised up) Man + fallen (cast down) Man; as knowledge is to good + evil cases.

Also, I see further variant games-talk to present itself as follows.

Here: paradox is to faces; as Totality is to Absolute Whole + natural World cases; as Man qua Christ is to godly Man writ large as transcendent God + ungodly Man writ large as transcended Satan cases; as knowledge is to good + evil. As a variant of Man as godly + ungodly, I see Christ to be sinless + sin-burdened as, respectively, pro-Christ + anti-Christ cases.

From which assorted language games, I see it that, whereas Hegelian games-talk follows orthodox Christian games-talk in championing good over evil, Atonism finds for good and evil having parity of esteem re: equal right-of-existence: by reason of paradox logic, faces of paradox – as thereby including good and evil – necessarily process in continual mutual eclipse; each, by turn, ceaselessly both triumphs over the other and is triumphed over by the other.

Conclusion

For Atonism, each identity in the story of the world – every case of A = A – is the Word as TC qua something (or that) than which nothing greater can be conceived. Each as games-talk is at once opposites, including divine + mundane natures, good + evil natures, ideal + material natures, ethereal + gross natures, Absolute Whole and natural World natures, and so on, for all paired opposites. Accordingly, Hegelian games-talk, like the games-talk of orthodox Christian Monotheism, is traditional Monism (there is but one Totality, one-only Christ). Such games-talk, like that of any other traditional monistic kind, is games-talk reaching towards voicing each identity in the world story to be a TC paradox, a TC atonement, an identity as dynamically two-faced.

This concludes Diary work treating with philosophies of the Modern period. I now move on to consider how philosophies of the Contemporary period fit with Atonism, starting with the thinking of Russell, as follows.

Notes

1. It could be said of the Christian doctrines of the Incarnation and the Blessed Trinity, respectively, that Christ and the Holy Spirit are not cases of paradox but are cases of mediation between an original One and its reflection – in the same sense in which the 'is' of the identity statement 'it is itself' is a copula signifying nothing paradoxical. Likewise, it could be said of Hegel's thinking that the case is that of the Absolute Whole as the Totality qua an original One manifesting qua actualizing itself qua Idea in the World qua Reality as the image of Reason. Here, the actualization (Christ), like the manifestation of the Holy Spirit, serves merely as a mediator function, as nothing paradoxical. By this reading, Hegel's philosophy is traditional Monism with the Christian story as orthodox Monotheism. In either case, paradox is ruled out. Atonism is offered as an

DAY 12: HEGEL

alternative games-talk of identity sense, an alternative games-talk to that put out either as Hegel's philosophy or as the Christian story. Atonism does not stop short at seeing reality as mind-made, the World as God-created. It offers additional variant games-talk. It sees mind and matter, like God and World, as faces of identity as paradox, identity as atonement, as TC.

2. In terms of the Identity Law equation A = A, I see Hegelian games-talk to present as follows. For Hegel, the games-talk presents as a closed (consummate) system. For Atonism, the games-talk presents as assorted language games, each bespeaking identity as paradox, atonement, TC.

A=A PER SE, TOTALITY AS ONE

A=A, WHOLE, ABSOLUTE AS ONE   A=A, NATURE, WORLD AS ONE

= =

IDEA   ORGANISM

A: IDEATING   A: IDEATED   A: ORGANIZING   A: ORGANIZED

CHRIST

GOD	MAN
=	=
HOLY SPIRIT	PERSON (SPIRIT)

A: FATHER   A: SON   A: MIND   A: BODY

DIARY OF ATONEMENT

DAY 13: RUSSELL

Today's Diary work will focus on aspects of the thinking of Bertrand Russell to see how these fit with Atonism.

Introduction

Against Hegelian Idealism with its talk of the One (the Totality, the Absolute), Russell commits to the Pluralism mind-set, conceiving there to be the Many ones and these as nothing ethereal. Against Kantian Idealism whereby phenomenal reality is mind-dependent in its being constructed by forms and categories, Russell conceives the units of reality (the irreducible constituents) to be nothing *a priori* determined. As with Idealism, so with Russell's Realism: the philosophy is that of traditional Monism (one-ism).

I shall see it that Russell's thinking – whether it changed or abided during his lifetime, and as assorted language games – presents as follows.

Russellian games talk

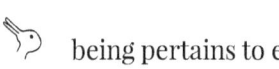 being pertains to every possible term or object, every conceivable case, including everything propositionally true or false, and to all such propositions themselves, also to whatever can be counted

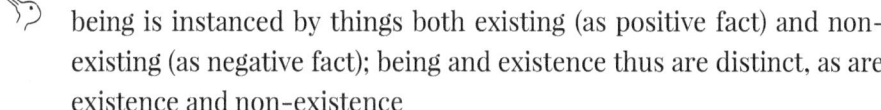 being is instanced by things both existing (as positive fact) and non-existing (as negative fact); being and existence thus are distinct, as are existence and non-existence

- Russell's thinking expresses as logical analysis and this as reductive analysis

- mathematics, science, and ordinary-usage language reduce to logic

- By Russell's general idea of reductive analysis expressing as the **Theory of Sense Data**, the basic constituents of reality, out of which reality (mind and matter) is a logical construction, are undefined (as such, they are not to be defined as either mind-independent or mind-dependent entities, nor as either anything psychical or physical) but are described as being discrete and self-subsistent entities

- as undefined – the definition thus left open – the basic (= irreducible) entities are wholly objective, neither one of any paired opposites

- an act of awareness (act of direct experience, act of acquaintance, sensation) relates with each of these entities, as subject to object

- where actual awareness occurs, the entities, as then subject-related objects, are called sense data; where actual awareness is absent, the entities, as potential-only sense data, are called sensibles (*sensibilia*)

- only sense data are directly experienced; sensibles (= unsensed sense data) are inferred

- a sense datum is simply a *this* or a *that* (plural: *these* or *those*) as an individual, be it an individual particular or (as a *thisness*) an individual universal

- a sense data case, at its simplest, comprises the sense datum: a particular thing possessing some or other universal quality or property, an example being *a patch of red* (= a *this* of *thisness* qua *redness*) – a qualitative quantum, or quantitative quality, so to say

- cases of *thisness*: roundness, colouredness, noisiness, odorousness, sourness, hardness

DAY 13: RUSSELL

 particulars exist; universals subsist (= have being as timeless entities)

 by Russell's general idea of reductive analysis expressing as the **Theory of Logical Atomism** – which goes beyond his *Theory of Sense Data* whereby the basic constituents are left undefined – they now are called logical atoms, called atomic facts, each as a particular thing (a sense datum, a *this*) with some or other quality or property (a sense datum, a *thisness*): for example a sense data case as a *patch of red* (sense datum + sense datum : particular + universal: a *this* + a *thisness* qua a *redness*) as the atomic fact

 a feature of Russell's *Theory of Logical Atomism* is his (use made of the) **Correspondence Theory of Truth**. Here, corresponding for their truth value with atomic facts are atomic propositions, an example of which is the assertion '*this is red*' ('*this is a thisness*') which denotes the patch of red sense-data case. Wherever correspondence does not obtain, the atomic proposition thereby is judged to be false

 by Russell's general idea of reductive analysis expressing as the **Theory of Types**, seemingly paradoxical (= contradictory) meanings are, properly, distinct higher-order and lower-order meanings (*for example, there is Russell's Paradox – a paradox discovered by Russell – which says that given the Class of all classes (none of which is a member of itself), if the Class is not a member of itself it paradoxically is a member of itself; this is seemingly a paradox which properly analyses out such that Class and class(es), respectively, are distinct higher-order and lower-order types of meaning, Class being a higher-order qua classifying type of meaning and 'class(es)' being a lower-order qua classified type of meaning; from which analysis, neither type is the other type; distinction (= dualism) is substituted for paradox and identity-sense as self-consistency sense is preserved*)

 more, re: the *Theory of Types*, in terms of reductive analysis as reductive linguistic analysis, types of meaning are language types, talk-kind types; here, the hierarchy – unlimited – is of languages

 by Russell's general idea of reductive analysis expressing as the **Theory of Descriptions**, the grammatical sense of language is distinct from its logical sense (*for example, the sentence "the golden mountain does not exist" – which has to it a surface grammar whereby the grammatical subject seemingly denotes an existent entity, viz., the golden mountain of which it is being said that it is a non-existent reality of some sort – analyzes out for its logical sense in terms of the translation: the propositional function "X is golden and a mountain " is false for all values of X' – by which reductive analysis the superfluous qua pseudo entity (the golden mountain) is discovered to be descriptive-sense only (a definite description); here, mountain and gold are not denotive terms: none denotes an existent entity; none names an actual existent object; the golden mountain vanishes*).

☞ by Russell's (use made of the) **Theory of Neutral Monism**, instead of there being the Dualism of subject-object opposite entities – which Dualism featured in such other theory as the *Theory of Sense Data* – there is the Dualism of non-same attributes pertaining to each (= monistic) ultimate constituent of reality, as a discrete, self-subsistent, entity: each one is a neutral stuff, the attributes of which are its psychical and physical opposite natures. Here, both mind and matter are logical constructions out of irreducible entities which are neither mental nor material but neutral. A case of a neutral stuff is the *patch of red* sense data (*this as a thisness*), of earlier mention

☞ by Russell's **Theory of Events**, and where associated with his **Theory of Solipsism**, the basic irreducible units of reality are events – one such being the (ubiquitous for this Diary presentation) *patch of red*, another being a state of mind as a psychical particular – yet with no demonstrative certainty for their existence, leaving it that solipsism (nothing for certain exists except myself), or solipsism of the moment (the whole of my knowledge is limited to what I am now noticing at this moment), though incredible, is a logical possibility

☞ by Russell's **Theory of Non Deductive Inference**, the ultimate constituents of empirical reality, the events told out by the *Theory of Events*, hence the logical constructions from these events, are known to exist with probabilistic (inductive) certainty – thereby avoiding solipsism. What justifies our belief in the existence of the external world and other

DAY 13: RUSSELL

people (these as the logical constructions) are, by hypothesis, principles of non-deductive inference. One such is the Russellian principle of quasi-permanence (= persistence) which postulates that there is a certain kind of persistence in the world, for generally things do not change discontinuously (say, a person – constituted by being the history of a series of events – changes from being an event qua a child to being a very similar event qua adult yet persists as the person)

Russell's Theories (assorted games talk) and Atonism

I see it that, to conceive of his various theories, Russell relies on opposite cases of thought, hence of talk. I shall see it by proposal that examples play out as follows.

Russellian Sense Data Theory requires there to the opposite cases of unknown being and known being (= unsensed being qua inferred sensible being and sensed being qua directly experienced sense-data being), also (re: knowledge) the opposite subject-object correlated cases (= acts-of-awareness and sensed-data correlated cases), also (re: sensed object) the opposite cases of particular and universal entities.

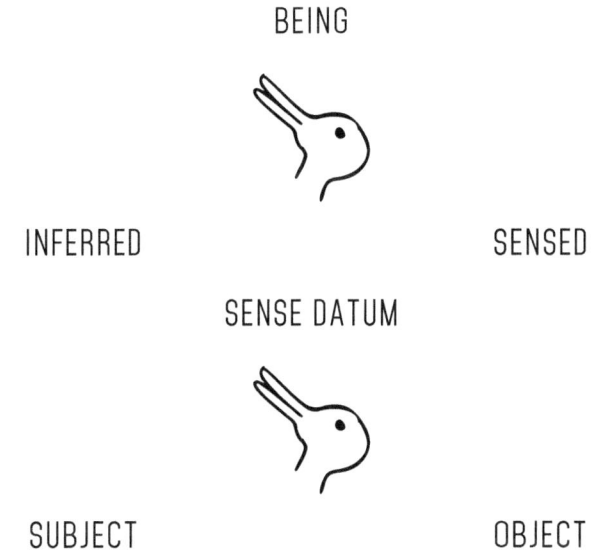

KNOWLEDGE

UNIVERSAL   PARTICULAR

Here: paradox is to faces; as being is to unknown and known cases (= unsensed and sensed cases); as each sensed case is to subject and object correlated cases; as each sensed case is to particular and universal directly experienced cases. By which proposed atonistic thinking, Russell's *Theory of Sense Data* is games-talk of paradox.

Russellian Theory of Logical Atomism requires there to be the opposite cases of atomic fact and atomic proposition as together truth-yielding correlated cases, also (re: the atomic proposition) the opposite cases of subject and predicate terms.

CORRELATION
PROPOSITION

ATOMIC PROPOSITION   ATOMIC FACT
SUBJECT   OBJECT

Here: paradox is to faces; as correlation is to atomic-proposition and atomic-fact cases; as proposition is to subject and predicate terms. By which proposed atonistic thinking, Russell's *Theory of Logical Atomism* is games-talk of paradox.

Russellian Theory of Correspondence requires there to be opposite cases qua corresponding cases.

CORRESPONDENCE

CORRESPONDING CASES

Here: paradox is to faces; as correspondence is to corresponding cases. By which proposed atonistic thinking, Russell's *Theory of Correspondence* is games-talk of paradox.

Russellian Types Theory requires there to be opposite cases qua higher-order and lower-order languages.

TYPE-TALK IDENTITY

HIGHER ORDER   LOWER ORDER

Here: paradox is to faces; as type-talk identity is to higher-order and lower-order talk-types; as (for example) classification talk is to classifying-type talk (say, talk of the Class of all classes) and classified-type talk (all classes, none of which is a member of itself, as Class-classified classes). By which proposed atonistic thinking, Russell's *Theory of Types* is games-talk of paradox.

Russellian Descriptions Theory requires there to be the case of description (as an identity) as that of opposites. By proposal: the case of description qua identity is as much the sense of description (verb sense) qua a describing-talk (= predicate-talk) as it is the sense of description (noun sense) qua a described-talk (= subject-talk); this is so whether the description be the case of an (ordinary language grammatical) sentence identity, or a (logical language) propositional form identity, or a (logical language) proposition identity.

DESCRIPTION,
GRAMMATICAL SENTENCE
LOGICAL FORM

DESCRIBING	DESCRIBED
NAME-DESCRIBING	NAME-DESCRIBED
PREDICATE	VARIABLE

Here: paradox is to faces; as description is to describing and described non-same talk-kinds; as grammatical sentence (say, the golden mountain is high) is to name-describing (golden, high) and name-described (mountain) cases; as logical form is to predicate (golden, high) and variable (X) cases; as proposition (as false) is to predicate (golden, high) and subject (say, Everest) cases. By which proposed atonistic thinking, Russell's *Theory of Descriptions* is games-talk of paradox.

Russellian Theory of Neutral Monism requires there to be opposite talk-kinds in terms of non-same attributes (say, psychical and physical).

EACH BASIC CONSTITUENT AS NEUTRAL

| PSYCHICAL | PHYSICAL |

Here: paradox is to faces; as reality qua each basic constituent qua identity as a neutral stuff is to psychical and physical attributes (which attributes, by logical construction, are such as mind and matter opposite natures). By which atonistic thinking, Russell's *Theory of Neutral Monism* (= a theory of monistic qua singular discrete neutral-stuff entities) is games-talk of paradox.

DAY 13: RUSSELL

Russellian Theory of Solipsism and ***Theory of Events*** require there to be opposite cases as follows. There are the rival Russellian logical possibilities: (a) the case of the Russellian singular qua solipsistic event (self-alone, the-present-alone); (b) the case of the Russellian non-solipsistic pluralistic reality (= events).

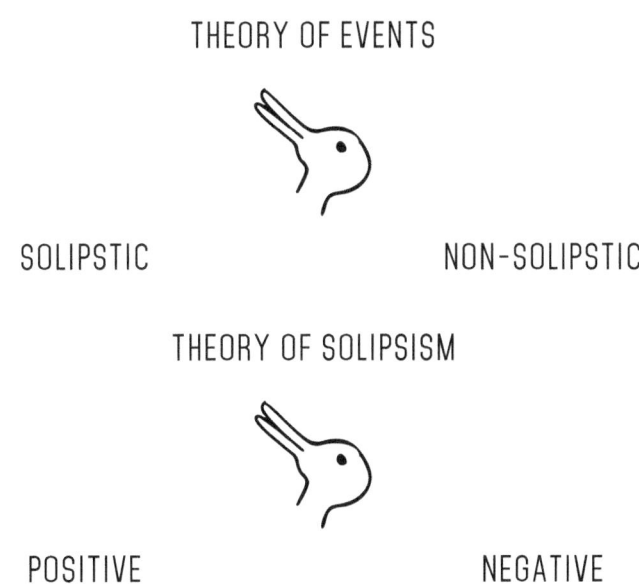

THEORY OF EVENTS

SOLIPSTIC   NON-SOLIPSTIC

THEORY OF SOLIPSISM

POSITIVE   NEGATIVE

Here: paradox is to faces; as the Russellian *Theory of Events* is to the (equally logically possible) solipsistic reality-event and the non-solipsistic reality-events; as the Russellian *Theory of Solipsism* to positive reality-event (solely the self, solely the present moment) and negative reality-event (no other-person, no external world, no past, no future) cases. By which proposed atonistic thinking, Russell's *Theory of Events, like Russell's Theory of Solipsism,* is games-talk of paradox.

Russellian Theory of Non Deductive Inference qua probabilistic (inductive) theory requires there to be these opposite talk-kinds: talk of an existent self and talk of an existent world; talk of probable reality being as much the case of lawfulness (= prescribed for by non-deductive principles) as the opposite case of lawlessness (= chance); talk in terms of a quasi-permanence postulate (= 'certain kind of persistence' postulate) of opposites qua non-same cases (say, personhood persistence throughout opposite childhood and adulthood states).

PROBABLE REALITY
QUASI-PERMANENCE

SELF   　　　　　　　　　WORLD
LAWFUL　　　　　　　　 LAWLESS

NON-SAME STATES

Here: paradox is to faces; as probable reality is to the probable self and the probable world non-same cases; as probable reality is to lawful and lawless (say, principles and brute matter) cases; as the postulate of quasi-permanence, or 'certain kind of persistence' postulate, is to non-same qua similar cases; as person is to adult and child cases. From which, Russell's *Theory of Non Deductive Inference* is games-talk of paradox.

Russellian Realism and Hegelian/Kantian Idealism opposite talk-kinds are these: Idealism and Realism; Kantian phenomena as *a priori* formed and Russellian sense data subjected to acts of awareness; Hegelian Monism (= the One qua Whole) and Russellian Monism (say, sense datum as each one of the Many sense data). The assorted language games presents in the following manner.

ATONISM

IDEALISM   　　　　　　　　　REALISM

ATONEMENT
SUBJECTIVE CONSCIOUSNESS

MONISM
(ONE OVER MANY)
KANTIAN A PRIORI FORMS

MONISM
(EACH ONE OF THE MANY)
RUSSELLIAN
AWARENESS ACTS

Here: paradox is to faces; as Atonism is to Idealism and Realism philosophies; as atonement is to One and Many (ones) cases (the Hegelian Whole and the Russellian Pluralism such as sense data); as subjective consciousness is to Kantian *a priori forms* and Russellian awareness acts. By which proposed atonistic thinking, Russell's *Philosophy of Realism* is a face-only of paradox.

Conclusion

For Atonism, the aspects of Russell's thinking qua games-talk investigated in today's Diary work shows a constant Russellian focus on opposite cases with an aim to reduce each case of opposites to a singularity – each singularity as an irreducible fundamental constituent of reality, leaving it that reality, as discrete self-subsistent constituents, is pluralistic (the case of Many ones).

For Atonism, Russell's commitment to the received thought form of Monism – whereby reality comprises Many ones – leaves out of account that non-same cases, as at once the case, are thereby the case of identity as atonement, as paradox. This commitment of Russell's accordingly prevents his thinking from seeing itself as an existent-only, a face-only of identity, and not an identity.

I see it that where Russell's games-talk thinking comes closest to voicing identity as paradox is in his *Sense Data Theory* – its seeing fundamental reality qua each case of sense data being at once a particular datum and a universal datum, also in his *Theory of Neutral Monism* – its seeing fundamental reality qua each case of a neutral stuff to be at once a psychical attribute and a physical attribute. For Atonism, the Identity-Law equation A = A is at once (= identically qua paradoxically) A/A non-same cases (= non-same terms) whether these be called non-same datums, or non-same attributes

Yet I see it that though Russell's games-talk comes closest in these two theories to voicing identity as paradox, his commitment to received Monism leaves his thinking resolved to reject seeing that identity is atonement, or paradox.

Nevertheless, for Atonism, in that Russell's whole thinking of Realism is seen to be a face of Atonism, a face of paradox, it thereby reinforces the thesis of Atonism, viz., the thesis that each identity in the story of the world – every case of A = A – is the Word qua something (or that) than which nothing greater can be conceived. By which thesis, each identity plays out as assorted games talk, including the games talk of Russellian Realism as a face of identity.

Having now dealt atonistically with the games-talk of Russell as an example of Contemporary Philosophy, I turn to a second example, viz., the games-talk of Wittgenstein, as follows.

Note

Nothing has been said in today's Diary entry regarding Russell's games-talk on religion or regarding his games-talk on good and evil. As I understand it, Russell was an atheist, or at least an agnostic, in matters of religion. As for good and evil, I understand it that Russell held these to be cases of real concern in the practical world and that only in the mystical realm, or the realm of abstract indifferent thinking, could the good and evil opposites be seen as merely apparent reality or be seen as of no great concern to a higher form of being.

DAY 13: RUSSELL

For Atonism, identity as TC is not identity as some mystical reality or some abstraction. Rather is TC all cases of opposites, including the mystical and the physical, the abstract and the concrete. Where Russell finds God and evil to be wholly incompatible cases, as contradictories, Atonism finds for them as opposite cases qua faces of paradox. Atonistically, talk of God and World (Man), or talk of good and evil, is games-talk bespeaking identity (TC) as atonement, as paradox.

I see Russell's games-talk to bespeak Monism and his games-talk of religion to bespeak criticism of Monotheism, including and especially Christian Monotheism. For example, his talk of there being no ideal One but only the Many ones (persons, things) making up the World, is a games-talk of Monism in terms of the one(s), rather than the One. Were we to regard Russell's Monism as the establishment view and in decree that the One is to be outlawed, we would see Russell's utterance to be the voice of God, the voice of good, railing against Idealism (including all things religious and mystical) as an evil spawned by irrational Man. In which case, whether for or against Russell, we would see the divine and the mundane, like good and evil, to be games-talk variants of (would-be or actual) establishment Man and anti-establishment Man, orthodoxy and apostasy, and these as opposite cases qua paradox-faces, where paradox features as the identity called Man, seen to be TC. This would be Man neither as mystical nor this-worldly, neither metaphysical nor physical, neither abstract nor concrete, neither ethereally divine nor grossly satanic, neither God nor Satan (writ small, respectively, as godly Man and ungodly Man), neither transcendently divine nor humanly fallen, neither good nor evil, but – re: all paired opposites – both cases at once, as identity qua atonement, as TC, existing as two-faced in the manner of continual mutual eclipse of opposites, as the dynamic interweave of incompatible natures, ever copulatory, howsoever moderately or violently.

DIARY OF ATONEMENT

DAY 14: WITTGENSTEIN

Today's Diary work will focus on the thinking of Wittgenstein – in respect of his works *Tractatus Logico-Philosophicus* (TLP) and *Philosophical Investigations* (PI) – to explore how the thinking fits with Atonism.

I begin by distinguishing between Atomism (to do with atoms) and Atonism (to do with identity as atonement); also between language games (as intended by Wittgenstein) and language games (to do with Atonism); also between picture-rabbit (as employed by Wittgenstein) and duckrabbit paradox (to do with Atonism); also between picture-talk (as employed by the TLP Wittgenstein) and out-picturing talk (offered in the service of Atonism).

TLP language games

By introductory proposal, I see it that the TLP text presents in criticism of traditional conceptions and findings of philosophy (see below). By proposal, the salient features of the TLP text qua games-talk, as commonly understood, put out as follows.

- The logical structure of language has surface (grammatical) sense and depth sense; by its depth sense is meant its true logical form; logical analysis discovers this form; it does so in respect of both language and reality; philosophy is a critique of thought via a critique of language; the target language is informative language; informative language comprises scientific statements; scientific propositions are statements of reality (science); reality comprises empirical facts, not things.

More: analysis targets propositions and facts at the atomic level; the atomic case is the irreducible foundational case; the atomic proposition exactly pictures – mirrors, represents, models – the atomic fact; the atomic fact is the combination of objects and the atomic proposition is the combination of elements; objects, like elements, are simples (indefinable); objects in an atomic fact – also called a state of affairs, as what is the case – fit together like links in a chain; the (factual) world is everything that is the case.

Too (of the non-factual world): the propositions of mathematics and logic are tautologies; tautologies, as non-informative (beyond the limits of informative language), are not TLP targeted; the discourses of metaphysics (including philosophical theorizing), ethics, aesthetics, also religion, are extra-lingual qua extra-scientific practices; extra-lingual practices qua scientifically non-factual practices, as non-informative (beyond the limits of informative language), are not TLP targeted; what cannot informatively be stated warrants silence; thatness (that there is anything at all) is something mystical.

Also: the proper function of philosophy is clarification of what properly does and does not make sense; traditional philosophy as explanatory theory makes no sense; its claim to do so is a misuse of language and is pseudo-philosophy – it is non-factual, hence non-informative; the TLP philosophy – its propositions – are cases of sense as cases of nonsense (discussed below).

This concludes the proposed presentation of the TLP text leaving, as the next task, a proposed presentation of the PI text, as follows.

PI language games

By introductory proposal, I see it that, as commonly understood, the PI text presents as revisionary: it does so by means of a revised method of philosophy; by this means it rejects previous conceptions and findings of philosophy including the earlier TLP text and its claim to be the final solution of all

DAY 14: WITTGENSTEIN 103

philosophical problems (see below). I see it by proposal that the commonly understood salient features of the PI text put out as follows.

 As a sufficient account of language, the TLP philosophy fails (the TLP philosophy of an ideal language; a reality-referenced language discoverable by method of logical analysis; a philosophy of a single, uniform account of the essence of language – an irreducible foundational essence; a picture theory of language, language referenced to something external to it, concealed by it; a philosophy which sees logic as perfect and grammar as imperfect); such philosophy is theory-only as but one of many different theoretical accounts; logical analysis of language (aimed to discover its true sense) is wrong philosophical method and enterprise; the proper philosophical method and enterprise is observation and description of language to discover (clarify, elucidate) its proper and improper conceptual employment.

 More: properly, philosophy is descriptive investigation of ordinary language, not explanatory theory of an assumed reality-referenced language; theory is a misconstrual (tantamount to abuse) of language sense – theoretical thinking is pseudo-philosophy; sound philosophy finds for language to comprise many and varied ordinary practices; grammatical sense is not unreliable (so the TLP view) but makes perfectly good sense to be trusted completely.

 Too: the many and different language practices are language games; these – like the games of life (cricket, snooker, netball, chess, hide-and-seek, and so on) have common as well as distinctive features; by analogy, language games are family members, bearing family resemblances (similarities and differences), each to the others; the sufficient meaning of a word is its directly experienced use, not (so the TLP view) its sense as a picture of an invisible essence; word meaning is open to view – simply look and see to observe its manifold usage; uses of a word in a language (game) are by further analogy employments of a tool from a tool-box.

 Further: language-game sense is a function wholly of the use of its words and their contextual circumstances; language games are interwoven into extra-lingual contexts; the interweaving, as the form of life, is a given; the given shows out as public criteria for language sense and life commonly lived – solipsism thereby makes no sense.

 Finally: philosophy as detailed descriptions of the endless variety of our linguistic practices is to be substituted for traditional philosophies (ontological and epistemological theories) finding for explanatory simple foundations; any finding is properly our own construction; apparent foundational objectivity (say, sense data), independent of the physical and human environment, is a consequence of traditionalist thinking; the form of life is criterial for all things linguistic and extra-lingual; it includes the admission of rule-following activity presenting as paradox (discussed below).

This concludes what I see to be the salient features of the Wittgenstein games-talk (the TLP and PI texts), from which I next offer an atonistic rendering of the salient features.

The Wittgenstein games and Atonism

Regarding the TLP output, I see it to present atonistically in variant ways, as follows.

ATONCEMENT, PARADOX
ATOMIC REALITY

PAIRED OPPOSITES QUA PARADOX FACES

DAY 14: WITTGENSTEIN

ATOMIC PROPOSITION

ATOMIC FACT

NON-SAME ELEMENTS   NON-SAME OBJECTS

Here: duckrabbit is to duck and rabbit faces; as atoncement is to paired opposites; as atomic reality is to atomic proposition and atomic fact cases; as atomic proposition is to non-same simple elements cases; as atomic fact is to non-same simple objects cases.

I see these three presentations to be in each case the presentation of a picture case as at once a picturing case and a pictured case. This talk is of what-is-the-case (the picture case) existing qua out-picturing in terms of how it is the case (a picturing case as a pictured case). Such games-talk I see to present as follows.

PICTURE

PICTURING   PICTURED

Here: duckrabbit paradox is to duck and rabbit faces; as picture is to picturing and pictured cases. The presentation is that of a triad (paradox + faces).

I next see it that the TLP games-talk speaks of such triadic sense as that which is the case – the case thereby of thatness. I see such thatness as indeterminate, as a foundational One which grounds the triadic sense.

ATONEMENT

THATNESS   TRIAD

Here: paradox is to faces; as atonement is to the cases of thatness and triad; as atonement is to One qua foundation of the Many (ones) and each of the Many ones constituting the triad (one paradox + one face + one other face); as Atonism is to non-same (One + ones) cases of Monism.

I see such Wittgenstein games-talk as a variant of the Christian games-talk treated with earlier in the Diary.

ATONEMENT
LORD

THATNESS   TRIAD
JESUS   INCARNATION

Here: paradox is to faces; as atonement is to thatness and triad cases; as atonement is to the cases of the foundational One and each grounded one of the Many; as Lord stands to the cases of Jesus the One and each one of the Many (the manifold qua triadic Incarnation: Christ as divine and mundane).

I further see it that the Wittgenstein games-talk is a variant of the Hegelian games-talk, also treated with earlier in the Diary.

ATONEMENT
SPIRIT, THE TOTALITY

| THATNESS | TRIAD |
| HEGEL (HIS PHILOSOPHY) | TDP |

Here: paradox is to faces; as atonement is to TLP thatness and TLP triad cases; as atonement is to the cases of Hegel philosophy and the TDP (triadic dynamic process); as atonement is to the cases of Hegel philosophy and the triad (the Total One called Spirit as at once the ever interchanging Absolute Whole One and the World ones qua persons and things); as Atonism is to non-same Monism cases.

Before leaving the TLP games-talk, this may be said. I see it that Wittgenstein considers the case of thatness to be the case of the mystical which shows itself but of which nothing can be said. In contrast, he considers all that can be said to be talk of the physical qua empirical statements of fact. He held that whilst science offers explanations it is not the business of philosophy to do so – in doing so, philosophy is simply theorizing pointlessly. He allowed it that his own TLP propositions of sense, as theoretical sense, were at the same time nonsense. I see it that the TLP games-talk puts out as at once talk of the mystical and talk of the worldly, talk of the metaphysical and talk of the physical.

This games-talk presents as follows.

TLP GAMES TALK

NONSENSE   SENSE

Here: paradox is to faces; as TLP propositional games-talk is to sense and nonsense cases; as TLP theory is to what cannot be said (the mystical, the metaphysical) and what can be said (empirical statement, the physical) cases; as atonement is to that which shows and that which is shown cases (including metaphysical subject + objective world cases, I + it cases, I + me cases.)

Coming to the PI games-talk, I see this as a variant of the assorted TLP/ Christian/ Hegelian, language games.

I see the PI games-talk to say that the given, as the form of life, is the varied assemblage of countless language games, each of which is the case of a word(age) and this as meaningful in terms of its usage. Each bespeaks identity as atonement, as paradox.

WORD

MEANING USE

Here: duckrabbit paradox is to duck and rabbit faces; as word is to meaning and use cases. The case, once again, is that of a triad (paradox + faces).

I next see it that the PI games-talk speaks of such triadic sense as a given (as the form of life) – the case thereby of givenness. Such givenness (like the TLP thatness) is indeterminate, as a foundational One which grounds the triadic sense.

ATONEMENT

PI GIVENNESS PI TRIAD

DAY 14: WITTGENSTEIN

ATONISM

NON-SAME CASES OF MONISM

ATONEMENT

TLP THATNESS   TLP TRIAD

Here: paradox is to faces; as atonement is to the cases of PI givenness and PI triad; as atonement is to the cases of TLP thatness and TLP triad; as atonement is to One qua foundation of the Many (ones) and each of the Many ones constituting the triad; as Atonism is to non-same (One + ones) cases of Monism; as identity is to non-same existents cases.

I see such Wittgenstein games-talk as a variant of the Christian games-talk treated with earlier.

ATONEMENT
LORD

GIVENNESS   TRIAD
JESUS   INCARNATION

Here: paradox is to faces; as atonement is to givenness and triad cases; as atonement is to the cases of the foundational One and each grounded one of the Many; as Lord stands to the cases of Jesus the One and each one of the Many (the triadic Incarnation: Christ as divine and mundane); as atonement is to the form of life and its multifarious individual expressions.

I see a variant of the games-talk thus far offered to be that of knowledge (in terms of human wilful experience) as both good and evil – again, a games-talk treated with earlier in the Diary.

KNOWLEDGE

GOOD   EVIL

Here: paradox is to faces; as knowledge is to good and evil cases; as (from earlier Diary work) Man qua human knowledge (experience) is to orthodoxy and apostasy cases; as Man is to establishment-applauded Man and establishment-reviled Man cases; as Man is to the cases of godly Man writ large as God and ungodly Man writ large as Satan.

Taking the TLP and PI games-talk together, I see it that the TLP games-talk is purist games-talk (to do with the ideal language) and the PI games-talk is worldly games-talk (to do with every day discourse). In this sense, TLP games-talk is idealist whereas PI games-talk is materialistic.

WITTGENSTEIN GAMES-TALK

IDEALISTIC   MATERIALISTIC

DAY 14: WITTGENSTEIN 111

Here: paradox is to faces; as Wittgenstein philosophical games-talk is to idealistic (purist) and materialistic (worldly) language games; as atonement is to abstract and concrete cases, perfect and imperfect cases, ethereal and gross cases, mystical and worldly cases, metaphysical and physical cases – where each games-talk (TLP and PI) sees the other as evil qua wrongheaded and sees itself as good qua right-thinking.

Whatever the variant games-talk, I see it to bespeak identity as atonement, as paradox. By reason of paradox logic, the faces necessarily process in continual mutual eclipse.

=
PARADOX
TLP ATOMIC CASE
PI WORD

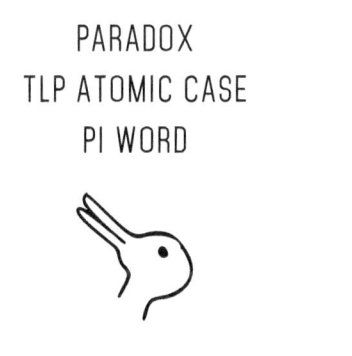

A   A

PARADOX-FACES IN CONTINUAL MUTUAL ECLIPSE
SIMPLES HANG IN ONE ANOTHER LIKE LINKS IN A CHAIN
FAMILY RESEMBLANCES RE: LANGUAGE-GAMES

Here: just as in the case of identity (signed in A = A by =) there is the interweave of the cases of A, as ever moving into and out from each other; so the TLP simples (elements, objects) hang in each other like links in a chain as the atomic case (proposition, fact); so the PI simples (meaning, use) resemble one another like family members – or like (toolkit) tool employment – as the word; so duck and rabbit faces interchange (are in continual mutual eclipse) as the duckrabbit paradox. In other games-talk: just as picture is as much a picturing sense as a pictured sense; so the TLP case (proposition or fact) is as much a simple picturing case (element, object) as a simple pictured case (non-same element, non-same object); so PI form of life is as much the case of living it as it is the case of it lived; so PI word is as much a simple picturing case (meaning) as a simple pictured case (use).

I next see it that just as a picture is a picturing case as a pictured case, or just as a case of eclipse is as much an eclipsing case as it is an eclipsed case, so a rule is a ruling case as a ruled case. So, for example, whether a rule is a 1 metre ruling of 1 metre ruled cloth, or whether a rule is a sepia ruling for a case as sepia coloured, or whether a rule is a ruling as a road which rules a case as (say) an ascent, or whether a rule of law as Lord is a ruling God as a ruled humankind – the rule itself (as identity, paradox, atonement, Lord) is neither the ruling case nor the ruled case but exists (out pictures) as both.

RULE

RULING　　　　　　　　　　　RULED

Here: paradox is to faces; as rule is to ruling and ruled cases. This sense is voiced by a Wittgenstein PI games-talk as follows. He remarks there to be this paradox: that no course of action is determinable by a rule; for every course of action conceivably accords with the rule. An ensuing statement is this: that whatever accords with the rule also conflicts with the rule. He concludes: there is neither accord nor conflict here.

I translate this cryptic sense as follows: no existent is identity, because every existent is identity; neither any duck nor any rabbit is duckrabbit, because every duck and every rabbit is duckrabbit. Each existent neither accords with nor conflicts with identity; each duck, like each rabbit, both is not and is duckrabbit.

Regarding other games-talk to do with the duckrabbit paradox, I concur with Wittgenstein in saying that I do not see the picture either as a duck or as a rabbit – rather, I straightforwardly see it to be a rabbit, or to be a duck.

DAY 14: WITTGENSTEIN

Wittgenstein says that the face seen like this (say, duck) has not the slightest similarity to the face seen like this (say, rabbit) – although they are congruent. This means – I take it – that the duck is entirely dissimilar to the rabbit though the two coincide.

CONGRUENCY, COINCIDENCE

OPPOSITES, WHOLLY DISSIMILAR CASES

Here: duckrabbit paradox is to duck and rabbit faces; as congruency is to cases not in the slightest similar; as coincidence is to entirely dissimilar cases.

Where I speak (in this Diary) of the duckrabbit as a duck face, or as a rabbit face, this is loose talking employed as a matter of convenience. I do not see the above figure *as this* or *as that* face. Speaking tightly, I see a duck, I see a rabbit, and I do this in the same way in which, with a coin in my hand, I see the head, and, turning it over, I see a tail. The head doesn't look *like* a head nor does the tail look *like* a tail – in either case it straightforwardly *is* what it is. This is a vital point. The above figure literally *is* opposites. Each exists in its own right entirely without the other. This talk opens the door to seeing it that identity is at once opposites – opposites having nothing whatever to do with one another. They are neither united, nor related, nor synthesized, nor in any way connected. They just are at once the case. The vital word is 'atoncement' and this as identity, atonement, paradox. (Note: Hegel never uses the word 'synthesis'. I see it that the Hegelian opposites simply are 'at once' the case. I see it that the Wittgenstein rule-talk makes the same point – cases without the slightest similarity are at once qua congruently the case).

Conclusion

I see it that the foundational games-talk of Wittgenstein bespeaks the TLP thatness, like the PI givenness, as the ground of what is the case (the Many TLP atomic cases, the Many PI language games – the Many ones). This I see to be foundational Monism grounding expressed Monism (the ones). Accordingly, for Atonism, the Wittgenstein games-talk bespeaks traditional Monism including its talk of paradox as singular cases of paradox (each atomic reality, each language-game word(age)). From which proposal, I see it that Wittgenstein games-talk is at once TLP Ideal Realism and PI Materialistic (this-worldly) Realism – these opposite cases as the paradox faces of identity (atonement, paradox) as Realism. In turn, as variant games-talk, I see such Realism to be a face-only of identity as atonement, an opposite face being (say) Hegelian Absolute Idealism. Whatever the variant games-talk, I see it that, for Atonism, each identity in the story of the world – every case of $A = A$ – is TC as the Word qua something (or that) than which nothing greater can be conceived, each as all things good and evil (and parallels).

This ends the Diary focus on Contemporary Philosophy games-talk as well as completes all of this Diary's work on Identity as Atonement and the case for good and evil.

Notes

1. I have included talk of Christianity in today's Diary entry, as well as talk of good and evil (cf. God and Satan), not least because, as I understand it, Wittgenstein was influenced by Roman Catholicism. Certainly, I see his triadic talk to have as a variant the doctrines of the Incarnation and the Blessed Trinity – each doctrine as a threefold games-talk sense.

2. I hazard the proposal that Wittgenstein, like Hegel, felt intimidated in that each wrote in the shadow of a great philosopher wholly committed to consistency as the criterion of rationality, hence of reality, being, identity –Hegel in the shadow of Kant, Wittgenstein in the shadow of Russell: Kant who rejected antinomy and Russell who rejected paradox, and that, for this reason, of felt-intimidation, each put out talk of paradox but in a manner replete with enigma and convoluted sense. Perhaps this is why Wittgenstein felt so wounded that Russell (in Wittgenstein's view) utterly misunderstood the TLP text.

DAY 14: WITTGENSTEIN

3. For Atonism, a variant games-talk is this: paradox is to paradox faces; as PI philosophy is to non-same cases qua TLP-commended philosophy and TLP-criticized philosophy; as atoncement is to ideal and gross opposite cases; as family resemblance is to equally non-viable cases; as ordinary language philosophy is to non-same cases qua the Rationalism/Idealism of Hegel and the Realism/Empiricism of Russell.

4. I see it that each of the three cases – Ordinary Language philosophy, Hegelian philosophy, Russellian philosophy – is that of a singular triad: word is to meaning and use; as Spirit is to Idea and Manifestation; as correspondence is to universal and sense-datum.

5. By proposal, the case of solipsism is that of a triad. The case is this.

ATONCEMENT CALLED ONE, SIMPLICITY, PICTURE

ONE-ING, SIMPLING, PICTURING   ONE-D, SIMPLED, PICTURED

6. As such, the case of solipsism bears family resemblances with all other cases of triad.

7. To rehearse with addition: by proposal, historically, Wittgenstein was influenced both by the outgoing Hegelian philosophy of the Age (Wittgenstein, like Hegel, a German speaker) and Russell's incoming anti-Hegelian philosophy (Wittgenstein, like Russell, a brilliant mind), as well as Wittgenstein showed interest in the Catholic religion – both its Christian Gospel (of identity called Christ as paradox) for the masses as well as for its purity of ritualistic form. By proposal, Wittgenstein favoured Hegel philosophy as a talk of paradox but not its focus on paradox content (say, Reason as Spirit as Reality). Rather, he favoured his own TLP text as a philosophy of identity as paradox with the focus on form, not content.

Here, according to this proposal, his target was the Identity Law form, A = A as the case of a simplicity (signed by =) of non-same simples qua A/A cases. I thus see it by proposal that, in this way, Wittgenstein steered unerringly between Hegelian paradox in terms of content and Russell's Monism. I see it that the spirit of the Age was against paradox such that Russell's anti-paradox stance influenced Russell to misunderstand the TLP work completely. I propose that such misunderstanding of the TLP text is quite understandable given its laconic and enigmatic style. But, against this as a criticism of the text, it equally may be proposed to its resounding credit that there is very good reason for enigma and succinctness. The text is doing business with pure form such that examples are impertinent. I further see it by proposal that it is for the reason that the TLP work is, as it were, a pure philosophy, and one which finds identity to be paradox, that Wittgenstein declared the text to solve all the problems of philosophy, and rule out as viable any other philosophy. He was giving out the Good News that A = A signed paradox, by which all sense is nonsense and all nonsense is sense. I propose that it is only for the reason that the TLP 'Gospel' was mistaken for a monistic perfect philosophy that Wittgenstein returned to philosophy to incarnate the TLP purity, its ideal, in the body of the PI ordinary-language text. My only reservation against finding for the TLP soul searching purity (also the PI work as its rounded off embodiment) as a magnificent Atonism is this: it stops short of Atonism in leaving the two works unremarked as at once the case, the case of (so to say) soul/body opposites qua existents-only, paradox-faces only, the atoncement of which is each person and thing as the Word qua TC.

DIARY OF ATONEMENT

DAY 15: TC

For this final Diary entry I want to look at ways of making sense of identity as TC such that it deals with the question: Of what practical use is it to entertain a games-talk of life as full of hope for happiness when evil lies around each corner? How does Atonism help?

I begin by saying that identity as the Word qua TC as something (or that) than which nothing greater can be conceived is not identity as greatness. TC is not something wondrous or beautiful or marvellous or amazing or at all a panacea for life's ills. Or, rather, it is each of these things provided it is said that it equally is the very opposite of each of those things. Equally, TC is not anything awful or horrific or fearful or dreadful unless it be said that it is each of these things as paradoxically the opposite. By which proposal, one cannot be human without equally being divine. One cannot be divine without equally being human. If one's entire life is torture this cannot be the case unless some other's life is altogether splendid.

Put another way: if I am Fagan I am Dickens. If I am Pip I am Dickens. If Iago, then Shakespeare. If Othello, then Shakespeare. In a childhood playground game, if I am a loser I am the Game. If I am the winner I am the Game. I cannot be the head without being the coin. If I am the tail I am the coin. Religiously put: if I am Satan I am the Lord. If God I am the Lord. In terms of a medical games-talk: if I have cancer I am the Play of Life. If I enjoy wonderful health I am the Play of Life. If there be a hero shaped from plasticine the hero is the plasticine. If from plasticine a vile stuff be formed that vile stuff is plasticine. As good I am evil. As evil I am goodness. As either of the two I am the Book of Knowledge.

In terms of Identity Law signed by A = A, I am =. I cannot say anything of myself as identity (as =) except in terms of A or A or AA – but in just these very terms I can say all about myself as identity, signed by =. I cannot exist as either A without existing as the other A but whichever A is the focus I am =.

As a yo-yo I am a toy, a game, a play. As up I am play. As down I am play. As play I am yo-yo. Road up is road down (so Heraclitus). Either I am good and evil or I am indifference; I am not a good versus evil combat; therefore I am an indifferent (so Hume). I say that I am neither good nor evil only by being both good and evil. The coin is neither and both of its faces.

To close. I see TC to be neither greatness nor leastness but both greatest and least because TC is play. I see it to be identity as the interplay of good and evil, each as necessarily existent. Such is TC as games-talk: such is the thesis of Atonism proposed in this Diary.

ABOUT THE AUTHOR

Bart Anthony Keegan, Ph.D., lives quietly in London pursuing his foremost interest: the philosophy of suffering. During his sojourns in England and Australia, he studied divinity and philosophy and began to question the meaning of life, the sense that theologians and philosophers made of it. This interest gradually focused on how to think about anything at all and the logic that is used as the tool of thinking. Bart met up with Anselm's proof for the existence of God and this changed entirely the direction of his interest. In that moment, he began to question if the way we think is in need of radical change from the root: the axioms of thought themselves.

The Diary of Atonement, *Poems & Prose of Atonement*, and *Identity as Paradox* are the fruit of Bart's questioning: They offer up as their thesis that each identity–person or thing–in the story of the world is an atonement of opposites: a paradox, from which, Bart came to understand that suffering, as sorrow, together with its opposite such as glory qua that which is glorious are cases as paradoxically one another, where their paradox case as their common identity case is neither one of them but both of them at once, and this (borrowing from Anselm) as that than which nothing greater can be conceived–identity-as-paradox as, so to call it, creativity as such. Each identity in the story of the world is a creativity, presenting either wholly negatively, wholly positively, or by turns each of these opposites. By which, that which is called the problem of evil–here called the problem of suffering–is accounted for as warranted by the justice of creativity as such, the fruits of which thereby are the cases of good and evil, glory and suffering, rejoicing and sorrow—the head-and-tail faces, so to speak, of the coin of untold measure that is identity as paradox.

Bart invites discussion regarding his work:
trabkeegan@talktalk.net

ABOUT THE DESIGNER

Elizabeth Beeton is a jill of all trades and mistress of none. Her life is mundane, made up of the usual things many humans experience: marriage, kids, ailing parents, aging, failing health, church, in-laws, outlaws, and scrabbling for a living.

She lives in Kansas City, Missouri, USA, writes novels, and is the owner of **B10 Mediaworx**, an author publishing services company. She designs print books, ebooks, and book covers. She publishes her own novels under the B10 Mediaworx imprint, and literature in a niche religious genre under the Peculiar Pages imprint. They don't make any money, but they are works that deserve a place in the Library of Congress. She builds and maintains her own websites.

She has a bachelor's in English, creative writing and journalism, from the University of Missouri at Kansas City.

She also reads, organizes her office endlessly, and tinkers on her computer (sometimes to ill effect). She's a fair-weather Kansas City Chiefs and Royals fan, half-arsed planner, avid cross stitcher, dilettante crafter, and aspiring odalisque. She regularly thumbs her nose at her to-do list as if it has any authority over her at all. Her life's goal is to finish all the craft projects she has ever begun. *All* of them.

b10mediaworx.com

www.ingramcontent.com/pod-product-compliance
Lightning Source LLC
Chambersburg PA
CBHW070201100426
42743CB00013B/3009